THURGOOD MARSHALL

The Fight for Equal Justice

The History of the Civil Rights Movement

THURGOOD MARSHALL

The Fight for Equal Justice

by *Debra Hess*

With an Introduction by
ANDREW YOUNG

Silver Burdett Press

For Sandy, who has always known that
all people are equal no matter how different they are

I would like to thank Della Rowland for her encouragement and guidance. I am also grateful to the NAACP, the Schomburg Center for Research in Black Culture, and the numerous civil rights lawyers in Washington, D.C., who were always available to fill in missing details; to Sandy Fritz, who reads everything I write with a critical but loving eye; to my parents Daniel and Susanne Hess for their love and support; and to my sister, Linda. A special thank you to Mr. Justice Marshall, whose life has been an inspiration for this book.

Series Consultant: Aldon Morris
Cover and Text Design: Design Five, New York
Maps: General Cartography, Inc.
Series Editorial Supervisor: Richard G. Gallin
Series Supervision of Art and Design: Leslie Bauman
Series Editing: Agincourt Press
Developmental Editor: Della Rowland
Consultants: James Marion Gray, Ph.D., Teacher, Lincoln Park High School, Lincoln Park, Michigan; Catherine J. Lenix–Hooker, Deputy Chief, Schomburg Center for Research in Black Culture, New York Public Library.

Published by Silver Burdett Press, Inc., a division of Simon & Schuster, Inc. Prentice Hall Building, Englewood Cliffs, NJ 07632.

Permissions and photo credits appear on page 122.

Library of Congress Cataloging-in-Publication Data

Hess, Debra.
  Thurgood Marshall: the fight for equal justice / by Debra Hess; with an introduction by Andrew Young.
    p.   cm. —(The History of the civil rights movement)
  Includes bibliographical references and index.
  Summary: Examines the life of the first black man to appointed an associate justice for the United States Supreme Court.
    1. Marshall, Thurgood, 1908—Juvenile literature.   2. Judges—United States—Biography—Juvenile literature.   3. United States Supreme Court—Biography—Juvenile literature.   4. Civil rights movements—United States—History—Juvenile literature.   [1. Marshall, Thurgood, 1908–
2. Judges.   3. United States Supreme Court—Biography.
4. Afro-Americans—Biography.]   I. Title.   II. Series.
KF8745.M34H47   1990
347.73'2634—dc20
[B]
[347.3073534]
[B]   90-32007
ISBN 0-382-09921-4 (lib. bdg.)   CIP
ISBN 0-382-24058-8 (pbk.)   AC

CONTENTS

INTRODUCTION

By Andrew Young

Some thirty years ago, a peaceful revolution took place in the United States, as African Americans sought equal rights. That revolution, which occurred between 1954 and 1968, is called the civil rights movement. Actually, African Americans have been struggling for their civil rights for as long as they have been in this country. Before the Civil War, brave abolitionists were calling out for an end to the injustice and cruelty of slavery. Even after the Civil War freed slaves, African Americans were still forced to fight other forms of racism and discrimination—segregation and prejudice. This movement still continues today as people of color battle racial hatred and economic exploitation all over the world.

The books in this series tell the stories of the lives of Ella Baker, Stokely Carmichael, Fannie Lou Hamer, Jesse Jackson, Malcolm X, Thurgood Marshall, Rosa Parks, A. Philip Randolph, and Martin Luther King, Jr.—just a few of the thousands of brave people who worked in the civil rights movement. Learning about these heroes is an important lesson in American history. They risked their homes and their jobs—and some gave their lives—to secure rights and freedoms that we now enjoy and often take for granted.

Most of us know the name of Dr. Martin Luther King, Jr., the nonviolent leader of the movement. But others who were just as important may not be as familiar. Rosa Parks insisted on her right to a seat on a public bus. Her action started a bus boycott that changed a segregation law and sparked a movement.

Ella Baker was instrumental in founding two major civil rights organizations, the Southern Christian Leadership Conference (SCLC) and the Student Nonviolent Coordinating Committee (SNCC). One of the chairpersons of SNCC, Stokely Carmichael, is perhaps best known for making the slogan "Black Power" famous. Malcolm X, the strong voice from the urban north, rose from a prison inmate to a powerful black Muslim leader.

Not many people know that the main organizer of the 1963 March on Washington was A. Philip Randolph. Younger leaders called Randolph the "father of the movement." Fannie Lou Hamer, a poor sharecropper from Mississippi, was such a powerful speaker for voters rights that President Lyndon Johnson blocked out television coverage of the 1964 Democratic National Convention to keep her off the air. Thurgood Marshall was the first African American to be made a Supreme Court justice.

Many who demanded equality paid for their actions. They were fired from their jobs, thrown out of their homes, beaten, and even killed. But they marched, went to jail, and put their lives on the line over and over again for the right to equal justice. These rights include something as simple as being able to sit and eat at a lunch counter. They include political rights such as the right to vote. They also include the equal rights to education and job opportunities that lead to economic betterment.

We are now approaching a level of democracy that allows all citizens of the United States to participate in the American dream. Jesse Jackson, for example, has pursued the dream of the highest office in this land, the president of the United States. Jackson's running for president was made possible by those who went before him. They are the people whose stories are included in this biography and history series, as well as thousands of others who remain nameless. They are people who depend upon you to carry on the dream of liberty and justice for all people of the world.

Civil Rights Movement Time Line

—1954———1955———1956———1957—

May 17—
Brown v. Board of Education of Topeka I: Supreme Court rules racial segregation in public is unconstitutional.

May 31—
Brown v. Board of Education of Topeka II: Supreme Court says desegregation of public schools must proceed "with all deliberate speed."

August 28—
14-year-old Emmett Till is killed in Money, Mississippi.

December 5, 1955–December 20, 1956—
Montgomery, Alabama bus boycott.

November 13—
Supreme Court outlaws racial segregation on Alabama's city buses.

January 10, 11—
Southern Christian Leadership Conference (SCLC) is founded.

August 29—
Civil Rights Act is passed. Among other things, it creates Civil Rights Commission to advise the president and gives government power to uphold voting rights.

September 1957–
Little Rock Central High School is desegregated.

—1962———1963———1964—

September 29—
Federal troops help integrate University of Mississippi ("Ole Miss") after two people are killed and several are injured.

April to May—
Birmingham, Alabama, demonstrations. School children join the marches.

May 20—
Supreme Court rules Birmingham's segregation laws are unconstitutional.

June 12—
NAACP worker Medgar Evers is killed in Jackson, Mississippi.

August 28—
March on Washington draws more than 250,000 people.

September 15—
Four girls are killed when a Birmingham church is bombed.

November 22—
President John F. Kennedy is killed in Dallas, Texas.

March–June—
St. Augustine, Florida, demonstrations.

June 21—
James Chaney, Michael Schwerner, and Andrew Goodman are killed while registering black voters in Mississippi.

July 2—
Civil Rights Act is passed. Among other things, it provides for equal job opportunities and gives the government power to sue to desegregate public schools and facilities.

August—
Mississippi Freedom Democratic Party (MFDP) attempts to represent Mississippi at the Democratic National Convention.

1958————1959————1960————1961

September 1958–August 1959—
Little Rock Central High School is closed because governor refuses to integrate it.

February 1—
Student sit-ins at lunch counter in Greensboro, North Carolina, begin sit-in protests all over the South.

April 17—
Student Nonviolent Coordinating Committee (SNCC) is founded.

May 6—
Civil Rights Act is passed. Among other things, it allows judges to appoint people to help blacks register to vote.

Eleven African countries win their independence.

May 4—
Freedom Rides leave Washington, D.C., and head south.

September 22—
Interstate Commerce Commission ordered to enforce desegregation laws on buses, and trains, and in travel facilities like waiting rooms, rest rooms, and restaurants.

1965————1966————1967————1968

January–March—
Selma, Alabama, demonstrations.

February 21—
Malcolm X is killed in New York City.

March 21–25—
More than 25,000 march from Selma to Montgomery, Alabama.

August 6—
Voting Rights Act passed.

August 11–16—
Watts riot (Los Angeles, California).

June—
James Meredith "March Against Fear" from Memphis, Tennessee, to Jackson, Mississippi. Stokely Carmichael makes slogan "Black Power" famous during march.

Fall—
Black Panther Party for Self-Defense is formed by Huey Newton and Bobby Seale in Oakland, California.

June 13—
Thurgood Marshall is appointed first African-American U.S. Supreme Court justice.

Summer—
Riots break out in 30 U.S. cities.

April 4—
Martin Luther King, Jr., is killed in Memphis, Tennessee.

April 11—
Civil Rights Act is passed. Among other things, it prohibits discrimination in selling and renting houses or apartments.

May 13–June 23—
Poor People's March: Washington, D.C., to protest poverty.

1 "MR. CIVIL RIGHTS"

❝ If we are wrong, the Constitution of the United States is wrong ❞

MARTIN LUTHER KING, JR.

The assistant hurried into the private dining room of the Federal Courthouse in Washington, D.C. He wasted no time—but walked straight up to Judge Thurgood Marshall and whispered in his ear. "The president is on the phone," he said.

"The president of what?" responded Marshall.

"The president of the United States" was the whispered reply.

Most judges live their entire lives without receiving a call from the president of the United States. Judge Thurgood Mar-

Thurgood Marshall, with Senator Robert Kennedy, before Marshall's nomination for solicitor general.

shall, 57 years old and a judge for less than four years, answered the phone.

"Judge Marshall," began President Lyndon B. Johnson, "the nation would be grateful if you would be willing to accept the office of solicitor general of the United States."

Marshall would later tell friends that when "the President asks you to go, you go." But when he first received the call, Marshall was unsure of what to do. The solicitor general is the third highest law officer in the whole country. He or she argues cases in front of the nation's highest and most important court: the Supreme Court. Although this was a great opportunity, it still presented problems for Marshall. The new position paid much less than his current one did. There was also the problem of job security. As a federal judge, Marshall already had a job for life. If he agreed to take this job, he could lose it in a few years. The position of solicitor general could be given to someone else by a new president. The year was 1965, after all, and few blacks were being offered important positions of any kind. Marshall would be the first black solicitor general in the United States. He thought about it for five days. Then he accepted.

Almost two years later, Solicitor General Marshall received another call from the president. This time, on June 13, 1967, President Johnson told Thurgood Marshall that he had chosen him to be an associate justice on the U.S. Supreme Court. It is an honor few people receive. Only nine justices sit on the Supreme Court. It is a job for life. Only when a justice dies or resigns from the Court is there a place open for a new justice. The president then appoints that new justice. The Senate must approve that appointment. A justice named Tom C. Clark had just resigned. It was now up to the Senate to approve the nomination of Thurgood Marshall.

Although the Senate approved the appointment of Thurgood Marshall to the nation's highest court, many people were angered by President Johnson's decision. A black man on the Supreme Court? Isn't it the job of the Supreme Court to interpret the Constitution? And didn't the original Constitution say that one slave was equal to three-fifths of a white man? Sure— that had been changed. Sure—they could vote now. But a black man on the Supreme Court? A man whose great-grandfather had been a slave?

When President Johnson announced the appointment of Marshall to the Court, he said, "Thurgood Marshall symbolizes what is best about our American society—the belief that human rights must be satisfied through the orderly process of law." In response to those who claimed the president appointed Marshall *because* he was black, Johnson responded, "I believe that Thurgood Marshall has already earned his place in history, but I think it will be greatly [advanced] by his service on the Court. . . . I believe it is the right thing to do, the right time to do it, the right man and the right place."

What Johnson meant by Marshall's "place in history" was clear to all who heard the president speak that day. Thurgood

Marshall had done as much in his 58 years to advance the cause of African Americans and democracy as any other person alive, including Dr. Martin Luther King, Jr. While Dr. King and others were fighting the battle against racism in the streets, Thurgood Marshall was fighting a similar battle in the nation's courts. As a lawyer he argued to change laws that were unfair to blacks. As a judge he interpreted the laws fairly. As solicitor general he argued in front of the Supreme Court to change laws. Blacks throughout the country had dubbed him "Mr. Civil Rights." Now, as an associate justice on the Supreme Court, "Mr. Civil Rights" faced a new challenge. As the first black on the nation's highest court, he would be interpreting the same document that had kept his great-grandfather a slave.

The highest law of this country is the Constitution of the United States of America. It is a short document that begins with the words "We the People of the United States...." These few pieces of paper were meant to bring together a nation whose citizens wanted only freedom and happiness for themselves and their families. But back in 1789, when the Constitution went into effect, not everyone was one of "We the People." The Constitution was written by a group of white men. They were "We the People." Women weren't "We the People." Native Americans weren't "We the People." Free blacks weren't "We the People." And the blacks who weren't free were slaves— slaves to "We the People."

Some of the men who created the Constitution wanted slavery abolished. So much time was spent fighting over this issue that everyone soon realized compromises had to be made or there would be no Constitution. One of the problems was representation. In the new Congress, each state would be allowed to have one representative for every 30,000 citizens who lived in that state. Since the southern states had more slaves than the northern states, they would have more representatives. This upset most of the people from the North. On the other hand, the southern states would also have to pay more taxes if each of their slaves were counted as one person. This upset many people in the South. The compromise? To count each slave as only three-fifths of a person. That way the South would have fewer representatives in Congress. They would also pay less in taxes.

The writers of the Constitution also set up the Supreme Court. Over the years, it has become the function of the Supreme Court to interpret the Constitution, to apply its words to everyday living. But as Thurgood Marshall wrote in the foreword to the book *Black Mondays*, "The men who gathered in Philadelphia in 1787 could not have...imagined, nor would they have accepted, that the document they were [writing] would one day be [interpreted] by a Supreme Court to which had been appointed a woman and the descendant of an African slave."

In the years since 1789, many people have challenged the words of the original Constitution. As early as 1856, a case was brought before the Supreme Court on the issue of slaves as "We the People." A Missouri slave named Dred Scott had been taken to Illinois and the Wisconsin Territory, where slavery was against the law. When his "master" took him back to Missouri, Dred Scott sued for his freedom, saying he had lived in a state and a territory where slavery was illegal. This, he said, should make him a free man. The legal question was whether or not Scott had the right to sue. The real issue was whether or not Dred Scott was included in the phrase "We the People." The decision of the Court was written by Chief Justice Roger B. Taney in 1857:

> We think [slaves] are not [We the People], and that they are not included, and were not intended to be included.... They had for more than a century before been regarded as beings of an inferior order, and altogether unfit to [be with] the white race...and so inferior that they had no rights which the white man [had]; and that the Negro might justly and lawfully be reduced to slavery.... [So] a

negro of the African race...[was looked on] as an article of property, and held, and bought and sold as such....

Almost seventy years after the Constitution had been written, African Americans were still considered property. The Supreme Court said so. The Supreme Court decided the law of the land, so it must be true. There was nothing that could be done to change the situation. Right? Wrong. Many people didn't believe that just because the Supreme Court said something, it had to be true. These people didn't believe that slavery was right. And they were willing to fight for their beliefs. Soon after the *Dred Scott* decision, the Northern and Southern states of the United States went to war against each other. The Civil War was fought for a number of reasons. One of them was slavery.

The Civil War began in 1861 and lasted four years. It was a brutal and bloody war. Hundreds of thousands of people died on both sides. A lot of property was destroyed. But in September 1862, President Abraham Lincoln made a speech that is now famous. This speech was called the Emancipation Proclamation. In it, Lincoln freed the slaves in the Confederacy as of January 1, 1863. It would no longer be legal to buy or sell an African American. The war was still going on. But if the Confederacy lost, Southerners knew that slavery would end. When the North won the war in 1865, Lincoln wanted to make slavery illegal throughout the entire country. It was time to change the Constitution.

Changes to the Constitution are called amendments. The way a proposed amendment becomes part of the Constitution is a long one with many hurdles. Only 26 amendments have been added in over two hundred years. Three of those amendments say that blacks have a right to be "We the People." The 13th Amendment (1865) ended all slavery in the United States. The 14th Amendment (1868) made African Americans citizens of the United States. The 15th Amendment (1870) said that neither the

United States nor any state government could keep citizens from voting because of their race or because they had once been slaves. In the years following the passage of these amendments, blacks joined the army, got jobs where they hadn't been hired before, and tried to vote. They were now "We the People." They were supposed to have all the rights that whites had. They were supposed to be equal.

Unfortunately, it wasn't only a matter of changing a few laws. In the hearts and minds of many Americans, African Americans were still slaves. Many whites refused to have anything to do with blacks. They refused to allow them to be equal. Equal, they said, but keep them separate. Give them separate public restrooms and separate restaurants, and there's nothing anyone can do. Soon, all across the South, there sprang up Colored Only and White Only signs. Even water fountains were marked with these signs. On southern buses, there were separate sections for blacks.

Colored, Negro, people of color, black, Afro-American, and *African American*—over the years in the United States, blacks, or African Americans, have been called by different names. Depending on how a word was used, it could be insulting or reflect pride. The names have changed as blacks' image of themselves has changed. By the end of World War II, many blacks felt a growing sense of pride about their race, and demanded to be called what they wanted to be called—Negroes. While some whites respected this, there were still many in the South who would curl their lips and sneer "Nigra," meaning it to sound as insulting as it was. In the 1960s, blacks began preferring to be called blacks. Toward the end of the 20th century, the term *African American* was introduced. But when Colored Only signs were scattered throughout the South, very few whites cared what a black wanted to be called. As a result, very few blacks were brave enough to stand up for their rights.

In 1894, just over 30 years after Lincoln freed the slaves, a man who was considered black only because a distant ancestor had been black was arrested for sitting in the whites-only section of a train. His name was Homer Plessy. The case before the Supreme Court was called *Plessy* v. *Ferguson*. Ferguson was the detective who arrested Plessy for refusing to move to a colored-only car in the train. The *v.* means "versus," or one side against the other. Homer Plessy's lawyer argued that providing separate but equal facilities was against the original meaning of the Constitution. The case remained before the Supreme Court for two years. On May 18, 1896, the Supreme Court said it was okay to provide separate but equal facilities for whites and blacks. The Supreme Court made segregation the law of the land.

It was going to be a difficult and painful struggle to change the way African Americans were viewed in the United States. But many people who had not yet been born would continue this difficult struggle. They would fight in the streets and in the courts to be equal. They would insist that people treat them with dignity and respect. Long before there was a Michael Jackson or a Jesse Jackson, a Daryl Strawberry or a Bill Cosby, there was a handful of blacks who refused to be shoved into the background of a country that would not treat them as equals. Dr. Martin Luther King, Jr., Malcolm X, and Fannie Lou Hamer were all part of the war against racism. Leading the battle in the courtrooms, there was Thurgood Marshall.

BUT LINCOLN FREED THE SLAVES

66 *The problem of the twentieth century is the problem of the color line.* *99*

W. E. B. DU BOIS

O n July 2, 1908, a boy was born to William Canfield Marshall and Norma Arica Marshall of Baltimore, Maryland. They named their baby Thoroughgood, after his grandfather on his father's side. But once young Thoroughgood learned to write, he got really tired of spelling out that long name, so he shortened it to Thurgood.

Thurgood Marshall's grandfather was a rough-and-tumble sailor who used two names because he never knew which one was the right one. He also used two names so that once he retired he could receive army money under both names.

Thurgood was pretty lucky. He could have been given his grandfather's other name: Thornygood. Or he could have been named after his other grandfather, a seaman, whose name was Isaiah O. B. Williams. The O. B. stood for Olive Branch, a symbol of peace. For a man with peace as a middle name, Isaiah Williams sure knew when to fight. Once, a snobby white neighbor who hadn't spoken to Isaiah for years unexpectedly asked him to help put up a fence between their two properties. Isaiah Olive Branch Williams told the neighbor, "I'd rather go to hell."

Isaiah wasn't the only relative of Thurgood's who was willing to put up a fight. Thurgood's great-grandfather, a slave, could be an ornery man. As Thurgood tells it:

> Way back back before the Civil War, this rich man from Maryland went to the Congo on a hunting [trip] or something. The whole time he was there, this little black boy trailed him around. So when they got ready to come back to this country, they just picked him up and brought him along. The years passed and he grew up, and boy, he grew up into one mean man. One day, his owner came to him and said: "You're so evil I got to get rid of you. But I haven't the heart to sell you or give you to another man. So I'll tell you what I'll do: if you'll get out of the town and county and state, I'll give you your freedom." Well—my great-grandfather never said a word, just looked at him. And he walked off the place, settled down a couple miles away, raised his family and lived there till the day he died. And nobody ever laid a hand on him.

By the time Thurgood's parents settled down to raise a family, slavery was a thing of the past. Being ornery didn't get you your freedom anymore. But it could get you into a good deal of trouble. As well-respected blacks in what was still a white world, the Marshalls practiced kindness and courtesy for their fellow human beings. They tried to teach their two sons to look for the good in people. But they also taught their children not to

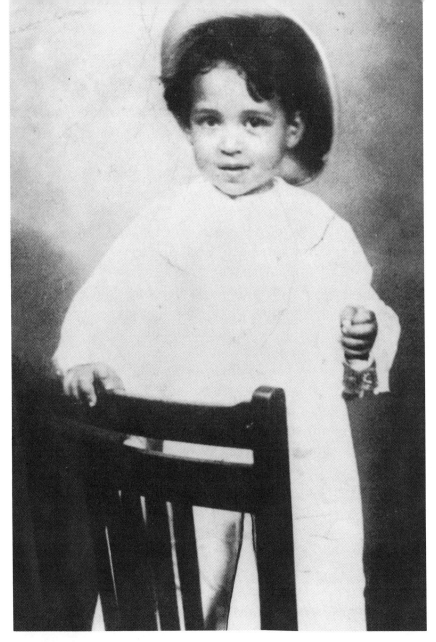

Marshall was originally named Thoroughgood after his grandfather. Later he shortened it to Thurgood.

let other people abuse them. "Son," Will Marshall used to tell Thurgood and his older brother Aubrey, "if anyone calls you nigger you not only got my permission to fight him—you got my orders to fight him."

Both of Thurgood's parents had been raised with a rich sense of black heritage that they passed on to their children. Yet they both had white ancestors. Thurgood's grandmother on his father's side must have been very light skinned because he didn't know if she was black or white. All his grandmother remembered was that she had been raised as a black in her home in Virginia.

The Marshalls were well respected in their Baltimore community. They were intelligent and educated people. Norma Marshall was an elementary-school teacher who encouraged her sons to think and learn. She also kept young Thurgood out of trouble. "Mama taught me a lot," says Thurgood. "I remember how she used to say, 'Boy, you may be tall, but if you get mean, I can always reach you with a chair.'"

Will Marshall was an amateur writer who worked as a dining-car waiter and later as a steward at a private social club for men. It was considered an honor to work at this club. Will Marshall was a proud man who often said that "he would 'sleep in the streets' rather than betray his principles." From his father, Thurgood learned a love of facts. They would argue for hours, the elder Marshall constantly challenging anything his son would say. "He never told me to become a lawyer," said Thurgood, "but he turned me into one. He did it by teaching me to argue, by challenging my logic on every point, by making me prove every statement I made."

Thurgood had a relatively happy childhood. He remembers his home as "warm and secure." He mainly remembers his youth in Baltimore as being spent out the back door of his house. "We lived on a respectable street," he says. "But behind us there were back alleys where the roughnecks and the tough kids hung out. When it was time for dinner, my mother used to go to the front door and call my oldest brother. Then she'd go to the *back* door and call me."

Both Thurgood and his brother attended the same all-black elementary school where his mother taught. With his mother's love of education and his father's zest for knowledge, Thurgood should have been a model student. But he was a mischievous and slightly wild child. As a result, he was punished often. The principal of the school punished Thurgood by making him go to the basement of the school and memorize a section of the Constitution. It became almost a daily ritual. By the time Thurgood left the school, he knew the document by heart. It had not yet occurred to him that he might have a career interpreting this document. But he did think it was odd that "We the People" and all the talk of freedom did not include blacks.

The summer Thurgood Marshall was born there were two days of antiblack rioting in the streets of Springfield, Illinois. Two men were killed that day. They were lynched—killed by a lawless mob. The men in Springfield weren't lynched because they had done anything wrong. They were murdered because of the color of their skin. They were murdered less than two miles from Abraham Lincoln's grave. Lincoln may have freed the slaves. But white America still wasn't buying it.

The lynchings brought national attention to the town of Springfield. It was such a brutal and unnecessary killing that it brought an outraged group of both blacks and whites to New York City. They attended a conference on ways to cope with the increasing number of racist incidents. The conference was held on May 30 and June 1, 1909. A group called the National Negro Committee was formed as a result of this conference. One year later, the committee met again and formed a new group. This time, they called themselves the National Association for the Advancement of Colored People. Everyone referred to them as the NAACP. Twenty-nine years later, a young lawyer at the head of the legal department of the NAACP would change the way the law looked at blacks. His name was Thurgood Marshall.

3

VIOLENCE, LUCK, AND WORDS

On the subject of the racial issue, you can't be a little bit wrong any more than you can be a little bit pregnant or a little bit dead.

THURGOOD MARSHALL

"**N**igguh," growled the man, "don't you never push in front of no white lady again." The stack of hatboxes turned, trying to find the voice that had spoken those words. The boxes were stacked so high that the body beneath them hadn't really seen anything. As delivery boy for a hat store, young Thurgood Marshall was used to boarding the trolley with a stack of boxes. Today, since it was just before Easter, there were more hats to deliver than usual. The hatboxes were stacked far above his head. Thurgood couldn't see anything. He could hardly see the steps he was climbing to the trolley. He

couldn't see the man who had spoken. And he certainly never saw any white woman.

"I was climbing aboard when a white man yanked me backwards," Thurgood remembered. Although he had no idea what was going on, the moment Thurgood heard the man speak, the moment he was called "nigguh," he dropped the boxes, whirled around, and faced the white man. What happened next was a blur of hatboxes and fists. Fourteen-year-old Thurgood Marshall did what no black man was supposed to do in 1922. He hit a white man. Then he hit him again. His father had given him permission long ago. No one should have to stand by and be called a hateful name like that—even if it meant going to jail.

As it turned out, Thurgood didn't go to jail. The arresting police officer knew the boy. His family was well respected in the community, and the white man didn't press charges. It was, nevertheless, a risky thing for young Thurgood to have done. In the 1920s, it wasn't unknown for a black to be murdered or jailed for life for hitting a white. In the Deep South, blacks were being murdered simply because they were black. A different police officer, a different white man, a different community, and who knows what might have happened to young Thurgood Marshall.

Growing up, Thurgood had to deal with a certain amount of name-calling and racism from local whites. It was never easy to hear the voice of hatred. Often, it meant making a decision whether to fight or swallow pride. Once, when his father got him a summer job in the dining car of the Baltimore and Ohio Railroad, Thurgood complained to the chief steward that the white trousers of his waiter's uniform were too short. "Boy," said the steward, "we can get a man to fit the pants a lot easier than we can get pants to fit the man. Why don't you just kinda scroonch down in 'em a little more?" As Marshall tells it: "I scroonched."

There was no one racial incident that changed Thurgood's life forever. Although his parents urged him to become involved with the growing civil rights movement, as a teenager, he was little interested in it. He was far more interested in hanging out with his friends. But even for a fun-loving teenager, it was difficult not to notice the unfair way that blacks were treated. Once, when Thurgood was in downtown Baltimore, he discovered that there were no public rest rooms a black person was allowed to use. He "felt the urge one day, hopped on a trolley to get home as fast as he could, and made it as far as the front door." It was an incident Marshall has never been able to forget.

Highlights in the Life of Thurgood Marshall

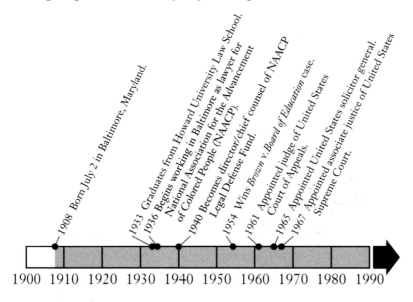

Although Will Marshall had given his son permission to hit anyone who called him a "nigger," Thurgood rarely used violence as a way of dealing with racism. He grew to be a large, powerfully built man—six foot two and 210 pounds. Because of his size, people were less likely to pick a fight with him. He also grew up to understand that choices must be made in life. If he chose to fight every person who called him a name, he would end up in jail or dead.

Eventually, Thurgood Marshall would choose to fight the war against racism with words instead of fists. He would come to believe that the basic structure of the American government could work for all Americans. As a teenager, he had already recognized the fact that a dead man can't fight any battles at all. Throughout his life, there would be times when he chose to play the game of black and white—especially when he was in the South.

As a young lawyer, Marshall once said about the South, "I know my way around. I don't go looking for trouble. I ride in the for-colored-only cabs and in the back end of streetcars—quiet as a mouse. I eat in Negro cafes and don't use white washrooms. I don't challenge the customs. . . ." Once he was in a small Mississippi town waiting for a train to Louisiana when "this cold-eyed man with a gun on his hip comes up. 'Nigguh,' he said, 'I thought you ought to know the sun ain't nevuh set on a live nugguh in this town.' So I wrapped my constitutional rights in Cellophane, tucked 'em in my hip pocket and got out of sight. And, believe me, I caught the next train out of there."

There were many incidents in Marshall's life when he made the decision to play by the rules of the game—even when the rules weren't fair. As a lawyer, he knew his legal rights. And he knew when to call upon them and when to "tuck them in his hip pocket." As a teenager, he knew when to punch and when to "scroonch." After finishing elementary school and high school in Baltimore, Thurgood was urged by his parents to go to college. At the time his prospects seemed "no better than those of his Negro classmates, many of whom failed to finish high school." His parents knew that the world could be a different place for a college-educated black man. His mother wanted him to study dentistry. It was becoming an acceptable job for a black man to have in those days. Dentistry was also a high-paying profession. Thurgood didn't know how he felt about being a dentist or about college in general. But he knew enough to listen to his parents.

In 1925, Thurgood Marshall went to college with the money his mother had gotten from the sale of her engagement ring. She thought he would become a dentist. He wanted to have fun.

4 LEARNING THE LAW

> **" [Blacks want] everything as of yesterday, because today is too late. They want to be repaid for everything that's been taken from us over a long period of years. "**
>
> **THURGOOD MARSHALL**

Thurgood Marshall was by no means an A student. Yet despite the years spent in the basement of his grammar school, he was accepted at one of the best all-black universities in the country. In September 1925, he enrolled in Lincoln University in Chester, Pennsylvania. Lincoln was a school with a growing reputation. Its all-white staff had attended the finest schools. Its all-male students came from every kind of economic background—rich, middle-class, and poor— and from as nearby as the next town and as far away as Africa. At Lincoln the students knew that they were part of a growing group of special men, a generation of educated blacks. They would be taught the same things that whites learned in college. They would know their rights and find a place for themselves in the white world. They would make the future brighter.

But before Thurgood got around to making the future brighter, he was expelled from school. In his second year of college, he was kicked out of Lincoln for "hazing" freshmen. Hazing is when older students who belong to a fraternity pull practical jokes on first-year students. Often the hazing is dangerous or embarrassing to students. As a result, it is not allowed in many schools today. That doesn't prevent some students from doing it. Fun-loving Thurgood took part in a hazing and risked the rest of his college education.

After a while, he was allowed to return to Lincoln University. According to some accounts, he was out of school for at least one semester. It was the end of Thurgood's troublemaking days. "I got the horsin' around out of my system," said Marshall.

The rest of his time at Lincoln was put to better use. He still liked to play cards all night and was the most outspoken at the bull sessions he joined in with fellow students. It was at this time that Marshall developed a love of debating. "If I were

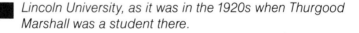

Lincoln University, as it was in the 1920s when Thurgood Marshall was a student there.

taking debating for credit," he wrote in a letter to his father, "I would be the biggest honor student they ever had around here."

Marshall was over six feet tall and weighed nearly 200 pounds. His friends said that he kept winning because he scared the opposition. They were afraid that if he lost he would tear down the place. But Thurgood knew differently. He spent long hours preparing for the debates, looking up facts and writing speeches. He was fast losing interest in dentistry. It was beginning to occur to him that he could make a living at debating. That's what a lawyer did, after all, he told himself.

For all his joking, Thurgood spent long hours studying. Of course, he made time for his friends. Once, when he and his friends were at a football rally, Thurgood jumped up on the stage uninvited. He delivered a 20-minute pep rally speech that brought the house down. The cheering, shouting, and whistling lasted long after he had finished speaking. Lincoln, which had lost every game but one that season, actually tied that game. Later, Thurgood said it was because of his speech that Lincoln had tied.

But college wasn't all studying. There were other ways to prepare for the future. One night, a friend of Thurgood's invited him to the movies. It wasn't unusual for a bunch of college boys to go to the movies. But this group of young men were all black. In the 1920s blacks were only allowed to sit in the balcony of the Oxford, Pennsylvania, movie theater. Thurgood's friend had something else in mind. He wanted to integrate the movie theater. The dictionary says *to integrate* means "to make something whole by adding or bringing together all of its parts." Integration became the battle cry of a nation of American blacks. It meant blacks could do what whites did. It meant Thurgood and his friends didn't want to sit in the balcony. Aside from the fact that the balcony was usually not as clean as the rest of the theater, it was harder to see the screen and hear the movie up there. Most important, though, was the fact that no one likes to be told where to sit. Thurgood and five friends piled into a car and drove to the Oxford movie theater.

The six boys bought their tickets and went inside the movie theater. The ticket seller nervously reminded them to sit in the balcony. They ignored her and took seats in the orchestra section. They sat up front, by themselves. Immediately, 20 more black students from Lincoln arrived and took seats around them. A few moments later, an usher appeared. He was a nervous 16-year-old who would rather have been doing anything other than kicking 26 blacks out of a movie theater. But this was his job. He told Thurgood and his friends to move. They didn't. He told them it was against the rules to sit where they were sitting. They continued to ignore him. Suddenly, there was a breath on Thurgood's neck. "Nigger," said a voice, "why don't you-all just get out of here and go sit where you belong?" When Thurgood had calmed himself, he turned around to face the speaker. "You can't really tell what that kind of person looks like," he wrote home after the incident, "because it's just an ugly feeling that's looking at you, not a real face."

Thurgood handled the situation with calmly whispered words. He told the angry face that he had paid for his ticket and was going to stay and watch the movie. He suggested that the man do the same. Then he turned around to watch the movie. A moment later, the ugly face behind him disappeared. So did the usher. After a while, Thurgood and his friends relaxed and watched the movie. Later they all agreed that it was a terrific movie.

The Oxford movie house was a fully integrated theater from that day on. Lincoln students sat where they wanted. Sometimes they wanted to sit in the balcony. But now it was their choice—not something they had to do because of white prejudice.

"We found out that they only had one fat cop in the whole town," Thurgood wrote to his father. "They wouldn't have had the nerve or the room in the jail to arrest all of us. But the amazing thing was, when we were leaving we just walked out with those other people and they didn't do anything, didn't say a thing, didn't even look at us—at least, as far as I know. I'm not sure I like being invisible, but maybe it's better than being put to shame and not able to respect yourself."

At Lincoln University, Thurgood Marshall discovered what millions of students all over the world have discovered in college—his own identity. He gained a sense of who he was and of what his place in the world would be. It was the 1920s, and African Americans were beginning to emerge slowly in various walks of life. He admired the singer and actor Paul Robeson and was challenged by the writings of W. E. B. Du Bois and other renowned African-American writers. More and more, he was remembering the sense of injustice he used to feel in the basement of his grammar school. He remembered reading the U.S. Constitution. He remembered not understanding why the rights of African Americans were never mentioned in the original Constitution. And he began to think that maybe, just maybe, there was something he could do about it.

During this time Thurgood met Vivian Burey. They met at a church dance and fell in love. He affectionately called her Buster. She was a calming influence and inspired him to study hard. Buster also helped Thurgood realize that he did not want to be a dentist. He switched his major from dentistry to pre-law and began studying harder than he ever had before. Everyone agreed that Vivian was great for him. "First we decided to get married five years after I graduated, then three, then one, and we finally did [it]," remembered Marshall.

On September 4, 1929, Thurgood Marshall married Vivian Burey. Thurgood, who was still attending Lincoln University, now had a wife to support. He worked as a bellhop, dining-car waiter, and grocery clerk. Between studying and his various jobs, Thurgood had little time for sleep. He spent any free time he had with Buster. He didn't know it then, but hard work and little sleep was to be the pattern of his life.

In June 1930, Thurgood graduated with honors from Lincoln University. He knew now what he wanted to do with his life. He would be a lawyer and "straighten out all this business of civil rights." But first, he had to be admitted into law school.

Thurgood's first choice of law schools was the all-white University of Maryland. Although no one actually told him so, Thurgood knew he was turned down by the school because he was black. He went to Howard University's law school in Washington, D.C., instead.

Howard University was the largest all-black university in the United States. It was founded in 1867 to educate blacks who had been turned away from the all-white universities. Harvard University in Massachusetts and a few other northern and eastern schools occasionally admitted one or two black students. But the southern schools had not broken their whites-only rule.

By the time Thurgood entered Howard, it was a changing school. The university's new president was also its first black president. His name was Mordecai Johnson, and he wanted to offer his students an education that was as good as that offered at any white school. From around the country he brought teachers to Howard who would become famous in the fields they taught. Among these men was Charles Houston, a man who would change Thurgood Marshall's life.

IRON SHOES

> *Justice is pictured blind and her daughter, the law, ought at least to be colorblind.*
>
> **ALBION WINEGAR TOURGÉE, author, lawyer, judge**

Thurgood Marshall entered Howard University's law school in 1931. He lived in Baltimore with his wife and traveled to Washington every morning. He would awaken at 5:00 A.M. and make the trip to Howard University in time for his morning classes. In the afternoons and evenings, he would study in the library. Sometimes he even worked in the library to help pay his tuition. It was a tiring schedule, but Thurgood loved it. Within a week of being at Howard, he knew this was what he wanted to do for "as long as [I] lived. I heard law books were to dig in," he said. "So I dug, way deep. I got

Thurgood Marshall's alma mater Howard University in the 1930s.

through simply by overwhelming the job. I was at it twenty hours a day, seven days a week."

In the beginning, Marshall studied general law at Howard. He took courses in all different aspects of the law. But there are so many different branches of law that a young student must eventually decide which to specialize in as a practicing attorney. Marshall took courses in business law, criminal law, civil law, and labor law. In his final year at Howard University, he took most of his courses in corporate law—law that protects businesses. To the outsider, it looked as if he might become a corporate lawyer. Marshall knew differently. Although he knew he needed to study corporate law if he were to open his own law office in the future, it was at Howard University that he "found out what my rights were." Thurgood Marshall was headed for a career in civil rights law, a branch of law protecting the rights of all people.

At Howard, Marshall met a number of brilliant and influential men. Of all those he met, none had a greater impact on his life than Dr. Charles Hamilton Houston, vice-dean of the law school.

Charles Hamilton Houston was one of the first black students admitted to Harvard University's law school. In 1919, at a time when very few blacks were accepted at any white schools, Houston had studied at one of the best law schools in the country. An excellent student, he was also the first black to sit on the editorial board of the law school's journal, the well-known *Harvard Law Review*.

At Harvard, Houston studied under the dean of the law school, Roscoe Pound. Pound taught his students what was then a new way of looking at the law. Until then, if a lawyer could prove in a court of law that a prior case was decided in a certain way, it would often influence the decision a judge or jury would make. This practice is known as *precedent*. Pound believed that although reviewing past cases was still important, the history, development, and problems of people should also be discussed. If past history has treated certain people unfairly and a lawyer can prove it had a negative effect on those people, Pound believed that such decisions could be changed.

Charles Houston saw this new way of approaching law as a key to arguing racial discrimination cases in court. It would be very difficult to find past cases in which a judge or jury voted against a white who had discriminated against a black. It would be much easier to prove that discrimination was harmful to the person being discriminated against. Houston also believed that if the legal system was ever going to change for blacks, black lawyers would have to be well versed in the Constitution.

If African Americans were ever going to make the legal system work for them, they needed to know what their rights were and how to make the law work for them. After completing his law studies at Harvard University and at the University of Madrid in Spain, Houston returned to his home in Washington, D.C., to practice law. It was then that he became a law professor at Howard University's law school. In 1929, Houston

Howard Vice Dean Charles Hamilton Houston was one of the first blacks to attend Harvard Law School.

became the vice-dean of Howard University's law school. It was time to educate the African-American lawyers of the future.

But the task of educating blacks as lawyers wasn't a simple one. James Nabrit, another law professor at Howard, said: "The real problem in those days was that we didn't have the facilities to argue these cases. We didn't have the lawbooks, we didn't have the [earlier] cases...we couldn't use the facilities or contacts of the bar [lawyers'] associations since they wouldn't let us belong." Another problem was that most blacks were too poor to afford law school even if they wanted to go. As a result, most of the students at Howard had full-time jobs during the day and went to school at night. Worst of all, the lawyers from Howard University Law School were looked down upon by white judges and lawyers. It wasn't just the question of color, either. The students at Howard didn't have the books or the teachers they needed to become great lawyers. Even if they had, they didn't have the time to spend on their studies at school.

So Charles Houston set about making changes. The first thing he did was to close down the night school. Save your money and then come to Howard was the message Houston sent out. Working all day and taking a few courses at night is not the way to become a great lawyer. Then he hired some new teachers and fired some who weren't quite as good as he thought they should be. Houston traveled throughout the country and brought back to Howard the most promising black students he could find. He may have angered some people, but his plan worked. Within two years, the American Bar Association (ABA) recognized Howard's law school. This means that the law school met the standards of the ABA and therefore became *accredited*. After that, the ABA began to accept the lawyers who graduated from Howard into their ranks. Howard's was the first all-black law school to be recognized by the ABA.

Of all the students Charles Houston taught, Thurgood Marshall was his most prized pupil. Houston was a demanding teacher. "First off," said Thurgood,

> you thought he was a mean so-and-so. He used to tell us that doctors could bury their mistakes, but lawyers couldn't. And he'd drive home to us that we would be competing not only with white lawyers but really well-trained white lawyers, so there just wasn't any point in crying in our beer about being Negroes. And I'll tell you— the going was rough. There must have been thirty of us in that class when we started, and no more than eight or ten of us finished up. He was so tough we used to call him "Iron Shoes" and "Cement Pants" and a few other names that don't bear repeating. But he was a sweet man once you saw what he was up to. He was absolutely fair, and the door to his office was always open. He made it clear to all of us that when we were done, we were expected to go out and do something with our lives.

Houston expected no more of his students than he did of himself. He held mock, or fake, trials, where students challenged the actual arguments he and others would make in court. In addition to running the Howard University Law School, he was also an active member in the NAACP. Although outsiders were generally not permitted to, Houston often allowed his prize pupil to attend NAACP meetings. Walter White, the executive secretary of the NAACP at the time, remembered Thurgood Marshall as "a lanky, brash young senior law student who was always present. I used to wonder at his presence and sometimes was amazed at his assertiveness in challenging positions [taken] by Charlie [Houston] and the other lawyers. But I soon learned of his great value to the case in doing everything he was asked, from research on obscure legal opinions to foraging for coffee and sandwiches."

Three years later and 40 pounds lighter, Thurgood Marshall graduated as the top student in his class at Howard University

Law School in 1933. He and Buster lived in Baltimore where Thurgood Marshall, lawyer, set up a private practice. Marshall and his secretary shared a small office decorated with little but a rug his mother had taken off her own living room floor. He had very few clients during that first year. The decade of the 1930s was the time of the Great Depression. People had lost a lot of money in the stock market crash of 1929. Although the price of food and clothes fell, people couldn't afford to buy these items because jobs were so scarce. People were poorer than they'd been in a long time. Some stood in breadlines for hours, waiting for free food to feed their families. Others kept their jobs but found little money to pay for anything other than food and their homes. Few had money to spend on a lawyer. "I did have one paying client," remembered Marshall. "The fellow used to get picked up quite a bit and the only thing he ever said to the cops was 'I want to see my lawyer.'... So then I'd come into the station and he'd say, 'Lawyer, how much they got on me?' I'm not saying he got off all the time but one thing was sure—he didn't hurt himself any by keeping quiet. And that's his right, no doubt about it, it's everybody's right."

Of the few people who actually hired Marshall, even fewer could afford to pay him. "One day I'd bring two lunches and the next day my secretary would bring two lunches and sometimes we'd be the only two people in that office for weeks at a time," Marshall remembered. His secretaries loved him, but admitted, "He had a genius for ignoring cases that might earn him any money." In Marshall's first year in practice, his legal business lost money—$1,000. The following year, Charles Houston was named head of the newly organized legal branch of the NAACP. Houston was preparing for an all-out attack on segregation. He wanted Marshall on his team, as the Baltimore representative for the NAACP.

6
WHEEL A-BOUT AND TURN A-BOUT AND JUMP JIM CROW

❝ *Equal Justice for All* ❞

On the U.S. Supreme Court
Building

One hundred years before Thurgood Marshall joined the NAACP, Americans were learning a new song.

> W'eel a-bout and turn a-bout
> And do just so.
> Every time I w'eel a-bout
> I jump Jim Crow.

Thomas "Daddy" Rice was one of the first white men to act out the part of a black man on stage. In 1832, he danced across a New York stage and sang "Jim Crow." It was the way he danced, the way he sang, that America remembered. Jim Crow was no ordinary man. He was a crippled black man who acted like a clown. He was someone to laugh at, someone to make fun of at parties.

By the middle of the 1800s, many whites thought Jim Crow stood for blacks and their "comic" way of life. By the time the NAACP was formed in 1909, Jim Crow had come to stand for the separation of blacks and whites. By 1934, when Thurgood Marshall joined the NAACP, the laws separating the races were known as Jim Crow laws. There were Jim Crow schools, restaurants, and public rest rooms. In a cotton mill in South Carolina, black and white workers weren't even allowed to look out the same windows.

In 1896, the U.S. Supreme Court had made segregation legal in the *Plessy v. Ferguson* case. Jim Crow laws were just another form of segregation. Many whites believed that the Supreme Court decision made these laws legal. Then, on May 13, 1931, a white NAACP lawyer named Nathan Ross Margold published a report on the unfairness of Jim Crow laws. The Margold Report said that this "separate but equal" system of laws was against the meaning of the Constitution. It pointed out that the *Plessy v. Ferguson* decision could be overturned.

Charles Houston was determined to see this law changed in his lifetime. With the Margold Report, he set up a plan to stop segregation, beginning with schools. Margold had called education the "soft underbelly of southern segregation." He called it this because it seemed to him that white southerners could accept the idea of integrated schools more easily than the idea of integrated workplaces, restaurants, or public rest rooms. Segregation was especially soft, he said, if attacked at the graduate and professional school level. There were several reasons for this. The most obvious was that segregation in graduate schools could be easily proved. Houston decided to begin with the law schools.

At about this time, a young man visited Thurgood Marshall

in his Baltimore office. His name was Donald Gaines Murray. He was a black who had just been turned down for admission to the University of Maryland's all-white law school. Marshall knew that the "separate but equal" law wouldn't work in this case. Maryland didn't have any black law schools. So if a black student wanted to attend a law school in Maryland, it had to be a white one. Marshall told Charles Houston about Donald Murray. In June 1935, they argued the case in a Baltimore city court. They argued that Murray had a right to study in any state he wished. Since the state of Maryland didn't have a black law school, Murray should be allowed to study at the University of Maryland. Houston also argued that forcing Murray to attend an out-of-state school was unconstitutional.

They won! Murray was admitted to the law school at the University of Maryland. It was a great victory for Marshall. The University of Maryland was the same school that had turned him down. "...They wouldn't let [me] go to the law school because I was a Negro," Marshall remembered, "and all through law school I decided I'd make them pay for it, and so when I got out and passed the bar, I proceeded to make them pay for it." When asked by a reporter if winning the *Murray* case was "sweet revenge," Marshall replied, "Wonderful. I enjoyed it to no end."

Marshall and Houston were a wonderful team. They spent much of 1936 traveling through the South and gathering information, looking for anything that could help them fight school segregation. They used Marshall's car as an office. "Charlie would sit in my car," remembered Marshall. "I had a little old beat-up '29 Ford—and type out the briefs. And he could type up a storm—faster than any secretary—and not just with two fingers going. I mean he used 'em all. We'd stay at friends' homes in those days, for free."

In 1936, Houston argued a case similar to the *Murray* case in Missouri. Lloyd Lionel Gaines, a black, wanted to go to law school at the all-white University of Missouri. The state of

Thurgood Marshall (fourth from left), shown with other members of the NAACP legal branch.

Missouri was so determined not to integrate its schools that it offered to build a law school on the campus of all-black Lincoln University in Missouri if Gaines would agree to apply there. If he didn't want to wait the years it would take to build the new law school, the state would pay his tuition at a law school in another state. Gaines didn't think either choice was fair. He wanted to go to law school at the University of Missouri.

Gaines lost his case. Marshall and Houston, sorry that Gaines had not been admitted to the University of Missouri, were excited nonetheless. They wanted to change what they felt was an unfair law. The way to change a law is to bring a case to the U.S. Supreme Court. The only way to bring a case to the Supreme Court is to lose that case in a lower court. The lawyer can then *appeal* the case to a higher court. If the case is lost again, it can be appealed to an even higher court. The highest court in the land is the Supreme Court. Because the Supreme Court receives appeals from many lower courts, the justices refuse to hear many of the cases that are appealed, choosing only the ones that raise questions about the Constitution.

Houston appealed to the U.S. Supreme Court. It took almost two and a half years for the Court to hear the case. But when the Supreme Court finally did hear the case it ruled in Gaines's favor. By 1938, the Court ordered the state either to admit Gaines to law school or to provide equal schooling within the state. It seemed that Lloyd Lionel Gaines was going to the University of Missouri. School desegregation had begun!

It was an important time for Houston and Marshall. The Supreme Court had ruled that a state had to supply equal education for whites and blacks. Did that mean that a state had to offer everything equal? All schools? What about hospitals? What about public rest rooms? Up until now they had been separate but not necessarily equal. Would there be an end to Jim Crow laws in the future?

In 1938, Charles Houston quit as chief legal counsel for the NAACP. In a letter to his father he wrote, "I have had the feeling all along that I am much more of an outside man than an inside man....I usually break down under too much routine. Certainly, for the present, I will grow much faster and be of much more service if I keep free to hit and fight wherever the circumstances call for action." Houston remained a part-time lawyer for the NAACP and returned home to his father's law firm. In his place, as chief legal counsel of the NAACP, he left a 30-year-old Thurgood Marshall.

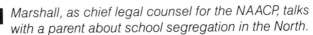

Marshall, as chief legal counsel for the NAACP, talks with a parent about school segregation in the North.

A
23-HOUR-
A-DAY
JOB

❝ *[Thurgood Marshall's] one of the special ones—a great rumpled bear of a man with the...dignity only those with a true calling ever achieve.* **❞**

Newsweek, June 26, 1967

Lloyd Lionel Gaines did not attend the University of Missouri. The state chose instead to quickly build a school at Lincoln University for black law students. Set up in St. Louis, Missouri, in an old building owned by a company manufacturing hairdressing, the school offered fewer law books and fewer teachers than the University of Missouri's law school. But during the years it took to argue his case and to build the new law school, Gaines went to the University of Michigan at Ann Arbor. He would have been the only student at Lincoln's law school. The new building at Lincoln closed down shortly after it opened.

No one ever reported seeing Lloyd Lionel Gaines after he left Ann Arbor. It was as if he had disappeared. For a while there was talk of foul play. But those who knew Gaines well claim he disliked being in the public eye so much that he may have chosen to change his name and live his life unknown to the general public.

Would Lloyd Lionel Gaines really have received as good a legal education at Lincoln as he would have gotten at the University of Missouri? Thurgood Marshall didn't think so. As the new special counsel to the NAACP, he was determined to see Jim Crow laws declared unconstitutional.

Based in New York, Marshall also kept an office in his parents' home in Baltimore. During this time, the NAACP focused mainly on segregation in the schools. But black teachers were paid so much less than white teachers that the NAACP decided to go to court over this issue as well. The first case concerned William Gibbs, a Maryland school principal. Gibbs's salary at the time was $612 a year. The average salary of a white principal at the time was $1,475. The case began on December 8, 1936, and took two years to close. But it was an important case for the NAACP. As a result of the *Gibbs* case and others like it, the NAACP won more than $100,000 for black teachers in nine counties. The NAACP also won 50 cases in different southern states and states bordering the South that guaranteed black teachers more than $3 million over a 15-year period.

The NAACP was constantly changing. In 1939, the legal staff became a separate organization called the NAACP Legal Defense Fund. In 1940, Thurgood Marshall became its first director. To many, the NAACP was a "stuffed shirt" organization—too formal and stiff. Marshall wanted to change that reputation. When he was younger, Marshall used to say that the initials NAACP didn't stand for the National Association for the Advancement of Colored People. Instead, they stood for the National Association for the Advancement of Certain People. At the time, not all "colored people" were allowed into the

Thurgood Marshall headed the NAACP Legal Defense Fund after his success as its chief counsel.

organization. "A redcap at Grand Central Railroad Station in New York had once brought more than 300 members into the organization," remembered Marshall. Redcaps, so named because of the red caps they wore, were porters who helped people carry their bags to and from trains. "Somebody proposed that he should be placed on the Executive Board, but other members were horrified. A redcap! What college had he attended? Who were his family?" It seemed that some of the members of the

NAACP were prejudiced against people who made less money or had less glamorous jobs than they did.

Thurgood and Buster Marshall now lived in a walk-up apartment in Harlem, New York. Thurgood worked long, hard hours. Buster kept the house clean, cooked meals, and talked over Thurgood's cases with him. Occasionally, they would go to a movie or be with friends. But for Marshall, there was little time for anything other than his work.

Marshall wanted the organization to work for everyone. So the first thing he did was to get rid of the stuffiness. The stuffed shirts were easy to find. "How very Tush-Tush" were his first words when he looked around the headquarters of the NAACP.

"You should have seen it, yeh, you should have seen it," Marshall told a reporter years later. "It was Dr. Whoosis and Mr. Whatsis and all kind of nonsense like that, bowing and scraping…you really should have been there. Well, I took a long look not too long but long enough and I figured I'd have to bust that stuff up pretty quick. Believe me, I had 'em talking first names in nothin' time and no more of that formality business. I was gonna relax and operate in my natural-born way and that's just what happened."

Marshall was often quoted as saying, "I intend to wear life like a very loose garment, and never worry about nothin'." But for a man who worried about nothing, Marshall worked non-stop to change the world. For the first seven years that he was the chief legal counsel, the NAACP filed a lawsuit every time it heard about a black being denied entrance to a school. "Isn't it nice that no one cares which 23 hours of the day I work," Marshall was quoted as saying at the time.

Marshall worked hard to change the image of the NAACP. He traveled about 50,000 miles a year, looking for ways the organization could help African Americans. Charles Houston had taught him how important it was that the efforts of the NAACP be understood and supported by the people. "Law-

suits mean little unless supported by public opinion," Houston had once said. "The . . . problem is how to create the proper kind of public opinion. The truth is there are millions of white people who have no real knowledge of the Negro's problems and who never give the Negro a serious thought." So Marshall became a lawyer for the common people. He listened to them and spoke their language. In a *New York Times Magazine* article, an NAACP lawyer was quoted as saying that "Thurgood is as comfortable at the Hogwash Junction function as he is in the home of a Supreme Court Justice." In the courtroom, he was serious and dignified, his great voice booming out points to the judge and jurors. In a living room, he was a guy with great stories.

When he wasn't in court fighting for an end to Jim Crow laws, Marshall was out on the streets with the people. He believed in the strength of labor unions and was even known to join a picket line or two. In Baltimore, he marched with steel-workers who picketed for higher pay and shorter hours. They marched so that children wouldn't have to work long hours in unsafe conditions anymore. Once Marshall helped a group of picketers who were being chased by the police in the pouring rain. He hid behind a row of bushes and held his breath for the cops to pass. "Wait until we get that Nigguh," Marshall suddenly heard a police officer say, "we'll know what to do with him." There was that word of hatred again. Marshall knew what the face that uttered that word looked like. Once again he saved his anger for the courtroom.

THE PAN OF BONES CASE

❝ We are not trying to make people love us when we go to court; we are trying to keep them from killing us. ❞

MARTIN LUTHER KING, JR.

The ugly faces of racism didn't belong only to those who called out names and killed. There were other ways of showing hatred. Thurgood Marshall and the other lawyers at the NAACP were discovering a kind of prejudice that existed within the law. Police officers were forcing confessions out of African-American defendants by questioning them for days while not allowing them to sleep, eat, or see other people. In some instances, the defendant would also be beaten or tortured. Finally, the defendant would become so tired, upset, and confused that he or she would confess to the crime whether or not he or she were guilty.

Involuntary confessions, or confessions that are forced and not given of someone's own free will, are against the law. Thurgood Marshall thought he could prove in a court of law that these "sunrise confessions" were as involuntary as if someone had been holding a gun to the defendant's head. He got his chance with the *Pan of Bones* case.

When three whites were killed in Hugo, Oklahoma, a black man was arrested and charged with the murder. His name was W. D. Lyons. For Thurgood Marshall, the name of Lyons would come to stand for a number of things. Justice was not one of them.

Marshall received a written account of the case from Lyons's lawyer, Stanley Belden. Mr. and Mrs. Elmer Rogers and their three children were at home on New Year's Eve, 1939. They were getting ready for bed when a bullet shot from outside the bedroom window killed Mr. Rogers. Mrs. Rogers ran outside screaming. Once outside, she was also shot and killed. In the dark confusion that happened afterward, the oldest son escaped with the baby. The middle child was still in the house. When the house burned to the ground moments later, the middle child was killed.

W. D. Lyons was not arrested until 11 days after the murders. He was then taken to jail, badly beaten, and put in jail for 11 days. He was then beaten again. This time he was beaten until he confessed to the crime.

At some later point, Lyons was driven to the scene of the crime by police officers. He was shown an ax and asked if it was one of the murder weapons. Afterward, he signed a second confession.

"It seems pretty clear," Belden wrote in a letter to the NAACP,

> that the reason they need the second confession is to show that Lyons was not forced to confess. They hope the second confession can be admitted as evidence. I don't think

they have a shred of evidence that doesn't depend on the confession, and if you could hear the full details of the torture which produced the first confession you would see why they don't want to rely on that. No jury could believe it was voluntary if they could hear Lyons. It will be nip and tuck whether they believe the police and the confession, or Lyons.

It would be up to Thurgood Marshall to prove to a jury that the police had beaten Lyons into confessing to a crime he did not commit.

The law was broken several times in connection with the *Lyons* case. An arrested person has the right to a lawyer. No one asked Lyons if he wanted a lawyer. According to Lyons, the police beat him. That, too, is illegal. Then there was the matter of the bones. Supposedly, one of the ways the police got Lyons to confess was by putting a pan of bones in his lap. Lyons was told these were the bones of his victims. He was forced to pick them up and touch them. But Lyons wasn't arrested until 11 days after the crime and didn't confess for another 11 days. Where did the police get the bones 22 days after the murder? If the bones weren't charred in the fire, weren't they buried by then? Once the story of the bones was known, the case of W. D. Lyons became known as the *Pan of Bones* case.

A charge of murder wasn't placed against Lyons until August 1940. A year after the crime, Thurgood Marshall arrived in Hugo, Oklahoma, to defend him. Much to his surprise, Marshall found an underground of blacks working to protect him. The blacks of Hugo and the nearby settlement of Fort Touson had smuggled in weapons from Oklahoma City and Tulsa. Marshall would go nowhere without bodyguards and would eat and sleep in a different house each night.

After a week of sneaking around, Marshall figured that people were going to see him in court anyway. With this in mind, Marshall left his office and started outside. It was in the hallway

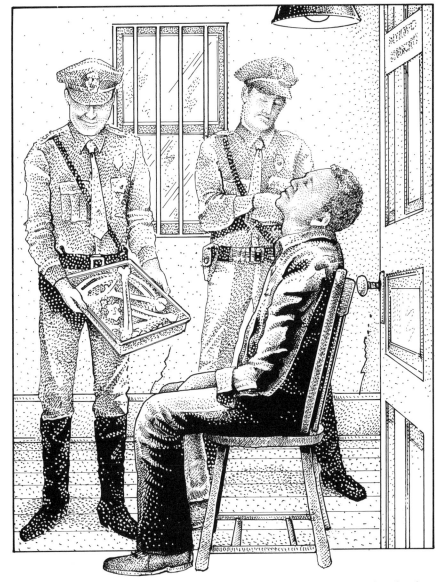

that Marshall came face-to-face with a white man who had a message for him.

The man identified himself as E. O. Colclasure, father of the woman Lyons was accused of murdering. He told Marshall that he had no idea if Lyons was guilty or not, but he wanted to be a witness. Colclasure said that Vernon Cheatwood, the governor's special inspector, had come over to his house on the day Lyons was arrested. Cheatwood had shown Colclasure a hand-held club called a blackjack and said that he had beaten a confession out of Lyons. Colclasure said Cheatwood had called the black-jack his "nigger-beater." Marshall was amazed. A white man, the father of the murdered woman, didn't think it was right that the police had beaten Lyons. And he didn't even know if Lyons was guilty or not. This was certainly a white man who was very different from the other southerners Marshall had met.

By the day of the trial, Marshall was prepared for the case. It would be his job to prove that the police were lying. To prove that they had, indeed, beaten a false confession out of Lyons. Marshall had all the facts. He even had witnesses who saw Lyons after he was beaten and witnesses who heard Cheatwood brag that he had beaten a confession out of Lyons. He also had a witness who had carefully gone through the charred remains of the house the day after the fire and found nothing. Three weeks later, the police claimed they found an ax in the same spot that the witness had gone over. In every state in the United States, a person is innocent until proven guilty. If all the members of a jury aren't absolutely sure a person is guilty, they cannot turn in a verdict of guilty. Surely all these witnesses would make the jury think twice. But W. D. Lyons was black, the witnesses were black, and Thurgood Marshall was black. The police force, the judge, and the jury were white. In 1940, blacks were not "We the people" in Hugo, Oklahoma.

The jury was sent out of the courtroom while the judge heard the first confession. They remained out of the room while he heard the evidence surrounding the first confession. After hearing the second confession, the judge stated that the first would not be allowed as evidence. But once the trial had continued in front of the jurors, the witnesses against Lyons kept talking about the first confession. The judge did nothing to stop this. Marshall had his work cut out for him.

Marshall and Belden knew they had to make the police slip somehow. They had to make them somehow admit that Lyons had been beaten. When Sheriff Roy Harmon took the witness stand, Marshall showed him a photograph and asked him to identify the people in it. It was a photo of Lyons being held up by two men. In the picture, Lyons was badly beaten. Lyons had told Marshall that the sheriff had been so excited about the confession that he had ordered the photo taken. Sheriff Harmon denied knowing anyone in the photo. But Marshall didn't believe him. Thrusting the photo in Harmon's face and pointing to one of the men in the picture, he asked:

MARSHALL: Do you know who this is?
HARMON: Looks a little like me, but there are several fellows here that favor me.
MARSHALL: Who does that look like in the middle?
HARMON: These Negroes look nearly alike to me, can't hardly tell them apart.

Can't hardly tell them apart? Marshall didn't believe that for a minute. A few moments later, he asked:

MARSHALL: Mr. Harmon, is W.D. Lyons in the courtroom now?
HARMON: W.D. Lyons? Yes.
MARSHALL: Can you point him out?
HARMON: Yes.
MARSHALL: Where is he?
HARMON: Sitting over there.
MARSHALL: I thought they all looked alike.
HARMON: You get to where you know them.
MARSHALL: But you can't identify him on this picture?
HARMON: That picture don't favor him anyway.

Marshall and Belden were up against expert witnesses. They were police officers and lawyers and knew exactly what Marshall was trying to do. They would do everything they could to see that he wasn't successful. They were doing a pretty good job of it, too, until it was the county lawyer's turn to question Lyons. That lawyer—Norman Horton—happened to be the one in whose office Lyons had signed the first confession.

HORTON: You say they brought you to my office?

LYONS: Yes, sir.

HORTON: And you say I was there?

LYONS: That is right.

HORTON: Don't you know that I did not come to the office until ten o'clock that night?

LYONS: You were in the office all that night.

HORTON: I was not in the office when you first came in, was I?

LYONS: You were there until they stopped beating me.

HORTON: I wasn't there in the office at six thirty, was I, when they beat you? (suddenly shouting) Isn't it true that Vernon Cheatwood had a leather strap and was tapping you lightly because you refused to answer the questions they asked you? . . .

LYONS: He had a blackjack and it was loaded.

HORTON: How do you know it was loaded? You showed no respect to the officers and just sat and sulked when I asked you questions, isn't that true?

. . . Isn't it true that after they got through hitting you, because you refused to answer their questions, I made them stop whipping you and told them to get out of the room, and I asked you if you wouldn't talk to me alone? Is that right?

Marshall and Belden were excited. There it was! Horton had not only referred to the beating and the blackjack, he had used the word *whipping*. "I made them stop whipping you," he said. And he said it before Lyons did. He used the word all on his own.

The trial went on for days. Colclasure, his son, and his daughter-in-law all took the stand in Lyons's defense. So did a hotel clerk who heard Cheatwood talk about his "nigger-beater." Lawyer Belden retold the story from Lyons's point of view— including Lyons's claim that the second confession had also been beaten out of him. When Thurgood Marshall made his final speech to the jury, he made much of the fact that Horton had used the word *whipping* and that Cheatwood claimed he didn't own a blackjack even though many witnesses knew he did. The trial was over. The jury left the room. All Marshall could do was wait for the verdict.

Later that afternoon, the jury returned with a verdict. "We the jury...do...find...W.D. Lyons...guilty of murder."

Thurgood Marshall kept working on the case while Lyons sat in jail. He worked on the case for three years. In October 1943, Marshall argued the case in front of the U.S. Supreme Court. Only the second confession was allowed as evidence. Marshall argued that the violence that brought about the first confession was still with Lyons when he signed the second confession. The Supreme Court did not accept this argument. It said that what Lyons went through before the first confession had nothing to do with the second one. In a majority decision of six to three, the justices of the Supreme Court said that the 12 hours between the signing of the first confession and the signing of the second one was enough time for Lyons to recover. Lyons was sentenced to life in prison. Of the 22 cases Thurgood Marshall argued before the Court as counsel for the NAACP, he lost only three. The *Pan of Bones* case was one of them.

Losing the *Lyons* case was a blow to Marshall. But it made him more determined than ever to fight for the rights of African Americans in the courtrooms and schools throughout the country. In 1945, one hundred NAACP members, mostly lawyers, met in New York City to launch an all-out attack on school segregation. The NAACP had already made some progress with the cases of Donald Gaines Murray and Lloyd Lionel Gaines. But the decisions passed down by the Supreme Court on those cases were decisions that affected only Murray and Gaines. Now was the time to convince the Supreme Court to make school segregation illegal everywhere. Thurgood Marshall would, of course, lead the way.

SEPARATE ISN'T EQUAL

> ❝ *Nobody needs to explain to a Negro the difference between the law books and the law in action.* ❞
>
> CHARLES HOUSTON, law professor

Once again, Thurgood Marshall and the NAACP needed a case to bring to the U.S. Supreme Court. They needed a black who had been turned away from an all-white school whose case would go all the way to the Supreme Court. It had to be a case that would reach the Supreme Court if the law of the land was to be changed. What the NAACP got was two cases instead of one.

The first case was that of Herman Sweatt, a black letter carrier who applied to the University of Texas Law School in 1946. The school accepted Sweatt but said that he would take classes in three small basement rooms set aside especially for him. He would be taught by part-time teachers. This would be a separate school for Sweatt, said the University of Texas. Separate but equal.

The University of Texas was clearly not offering Herman Sweatt an equal education. So the NAACP was asked to handle the case. A surprising twist came in the way the white students behaved. More than two hundred of them set up an NAACP branch on the campus of the university to raise enough money to cover Herman Sweatt's legal fees. So unlikely a sight was this in the Deep South that when a police officer appeared across the street, the students were sure they were going to be arrested. The officer watched them for a while as they tried to raise money. Finally he crossed the street and approached them. "If you kids want that 'cullerd' man in your school so bad," he said, "you sure got a right to have him." Then he dug into his pocket and handed them five dollars. Before the trial began, two thousand students from the University of Texas gathered for a rally in support of Herman Sweatt. When the president of the student body made a speech calling for the university to "practice the democracy it preached," the students cheered.

As Marshall had hoped, Sweatt lost the case in the lower court. It took five years, until 1950, for Herman Sweatt's case to reach the Supreme Court. Another case of Marshall's reached the Supreme Court the same day—the case of a teacher, G.W. McLaurin.

G.W. McLaurin had been turned down by the University of Oklahoma. At 68 years old, McLaurin had already received a college degree and had a successful career as a teacher. Now he wanted to study to receive an even higher degree—a doctorate in education. The court that had decided his case had ordered the university "to provide [McLaurin] with the education he seeks as soon as it does for applicants of any other group."

But when McLaurin went to the University of Oklahoma, he had to sit at a desk surrounded by a railing. The sign on the

desk read Reserved for Colored. Separate but equal? Marshall didn't think so.

In his speech before the Supreme Court, Marshall spoke of the way McLaurin was receiving an "equal" education. "He must sit by himself, outside the door of the classroom. He studies at a separate desk at the library, hidden by half a carload of newspapers. His dining room is a small dingy space known as 'The Jug,' and he eats conversationless and alone. The only purpose of this inhuman treatment is to [show] that McLaurin is an inferior being and altogether unfit to associate with the white race."

On June 5, 1950, the Supreme Court decided in McLaurin's favor! Under the 14th Amendment, said the Court, if McLaurin was accepted at the school, he must receive equal treatment. It was a victorious day for the NAACP. First, the Court had said that Murray and Gaines had to be admitted into graduate schools. Now, the Court was saying that all black students not only had to be admitted, but also had to receive equal education. Black students would now be able to go to graduate schools in the South knowing that they had a legal right to be treated equally. Of course there would be some who refused to treat them that way. But with the law behind them, they could hold their heads high. Step by step, Marshall and the NAACP were getting closer to reaching their goal of completely desegregated schools at every level of education.

The case of Herman Sweatt took the issue even one step further. Eleven southern states had joined together and filed a combined opinion (called a *brief*). They called for the Court to uphold the *Plessy* v. *Ferguson* decision of 1896. Providing separate but equal public facilities had been made law by the Supreme Court, they said. The Supreme Court should stick to its own decisions. But in a totally unexpected move, the Justice Department of the United States filed a brief for both the *Sweatt* and *McLaurin* cases. The *Plessy* decision was wrong, said the brief. It should be overruled. Overturning the *Plessy* decision was the dream of Charles Houston and Thurgood Marshall. It was too good to be true.

But it really was too good to be true. The Supreme Court did not follow the Justice Department's recommendation and overturn the *Plessy* decision. However, it did say that providing separate but equal public facilities was a law that had to be followed. It also said that separate education that was not equal was unconstitutional. From this point on, any graduate school that tried to set up a separate school for black students had better be sure that the education it provided was equal. Within a year, more than a thousand black students were accepted into white graduate schools.

On April 22, 1950, Charles Hamilton Houston died. Thurgood Marshall was one of the pallbearers at his funeral. Houston's friends and associates were now more determined than ever to carry on the fight he had begun. On his deathbed, Houston spoke with friend, colleague, and future Howard University president James M. Nabrit. He wanted Nabrit to carry on a group of cases involving schoolchildren who were receiving separate but definitely not equal educations.

Nabrit agreed to take the cases, but with a condition. He told Houston, "You know, for the last three years, Charlie, I have been trying to get you all to agree that you would take these cases and fight them on the grounds that segregation itself is unconstitutional.... If I take these cases I am telling you now that I am going to abandon this separate-but-equal theory you have...I am going to try these cases on the theory that segregation [itself] is unconstitutional."

Houston was pleased. "I'm glad to hear you [say] that," he told Nabrit. "Cause I'll rest better...I've about come to that position myself."

Houston wasn't the only one to come around to Nabrit's way of thinking. Thurgood Marshall had been thinking along exactly those same lines. Just after the *Sweatt* and *McLaurin* cases were decided, Marshall called a meeting of the Legal Defense

James Nabrit (right), the second black president of Howard University, with Thurgood Marshall.

Fund. Was this the time to challenge the *Plessy* decision? After much discussion, the leaders of the fund decided to continue to take it one step at a time. The first step was to attack *Plessy* on two fronts. The NAACP would continue to attack segregation in the schools. But they would also argue that to be truly equal, schools needed to integrate. Separate but equal public facilities just weren't good enough. The NAACP united in this effort. Its offices in every state began collecting evidence to prove that separate can never really be equal.

Even Marshall himself spent as much time as he could traveling in the South looking for evidence. This was something Marshall did from time to time throughout his career with the NAACP. It was often an upsetting experience for him. During one of these trips to the South, Marshall recalled:

There was no place to eat and no place to sleep. We slept in the car and we ate fruit. One place in Mississippi, we were eating and talking to people and a little kid, I guess 12 or 14, a little bright-eyed kid saw that I was eating an orange. I said, "Hey, you want one of these?" He said, "Yeah." So I gave him one and he just bit into it. He didn't peel it. You know why? It was the first time he had ever seen an orange. That will tell you what we had in those days.

As time went on and Marshall and the NAACP gathered more information, they began to realize where to launch their next attack: the nation's elementary schools. In 1952, the state of North Carolina spent $152 per year to educate each white child. Only $129 was spent for each black student. Mississippi spent $117 for each white student and $45 for each black child. In the state of South Carolina, the county of Clarendon outdid them all. While there were almost three times as many children in the all-black elementary schools as in the all-white schools, the white children received more than 60 percent of the money put aside for education. That translated into $179 per year for each white student and only $43 per year for each black student. What was equal about that?

DOLLS, WAR, AND TAR-PAPER SHACKS

❝You've got to be taught before it's too late.
Before you are six or seven or eight.
To hate all the people your relatives hate
You've got to be carefully taught. ❞

From the musical *South Pacific*

Thurgood Marshall didn't have to go looking for trouble in Clarendon County, South Carolina. Trouble came to him.

Harry Briggs was a 34-year-old black man who lived in Clarendon County. The father of five, he was tired of seeing his children receive an education inferior to that which was provided for white children in the same county. So Briggs and 19 other black parents in Clarendon County signed a suit that the NAACP brought against the school board.

People were fired for signing that suit. Stores refused to sell supplies to farmers who supported the cause. Harry Briggs's wife Liza remembers working at the Summerton Motel at the time:

> The White Council of Summerton came down and told [my boss] if he didn't fire the women who signed the petition that they would close the business down. They wouldn't let the trucks come and deliver. So they called us in and asked...that we take our names off the petition in order to work....I told him "no," I didn't want to do that because we would be hurting the children, and I'd rather give up my job and keep my name on there. So in about two weeks' time I was fired. Not only me, the rest of them who had anything to do with the petition, they all was fired.

It was up to the NAACP to prove that separating white and black children was harmful to the children involved. Against the advice of some of the other NAACP lawyers, Thurgood Marshall called on Kenneth B. Clark.

Clark was a black psychologist who for several years had been studying the effects segregation had on children. What made the other NAACP lawyers nervous was the way Clark was going about studying the children. He was using black dolls and white dolls. The lawyers feared they would be laughed out of the courtroom. Thurgood Marshall disagreed. He believed that the doll experiments showed exactly what he wanted to prove—that separating black students from white students would make the black children feel as if they weren't as good as the white ones.

Marshall, Clark, and another NAACP lawyer named Robert Carter took the train from New York City to Clarendon

County, South Carolina. Once there, Clark went to a combined elementary school and high school called Scott's Branch. It was, of course, a black-only school. Clark brought his dolls with him.

Clark's method was simple. As he had done before with younger children, he showed each child a black doll and a white doll. Once the children had shown that they could tell the difference between the two dolls, Clark asked a series of questions like this:

1. Give me the doll that you like best.
2. Give me the doll that is the nice doll.
3. Give me the doll that looks bad.
4. Give me the doll that is a nice color.
5. Show me the doll that is most like you.

Of the 16 children whom Clark tested, 10 of them said they liked the white doll better. Eleven of them thought the black doll looked "bad." Nine of them said the white doll looked "nice." "The most disturbing question," Clark said, "and the one that made me...upset—was the final question." Seven of the 16 children said the doll that was most like them was the white doll.

What was equally as disturbing to Clark was the similarity in the results of testing with children of a different age. The children tested in Clarendon County were six to nine years old. But in a previous test, with children aged three to seven years old, the results were the same. In the case of the younger kids, Clark remembered, "One little girl who had shown a clear preference for the white doll and who described the brown doll as 'ugly' and 'dirty' broke into...tears when she was asked [which doll was most like her]."

The results were clear. If you separate children because of the way they look, you are telling them they are inferior. "Segregation was, is, the way in which a society tells a group of human beings that they are inferior to other groups of human beings in the society," said Clark. If children cannot go to schools that are clearly better than the ones they go to, how are they supposed to feel about themselves?

The three-judge district court that heard the case did not agree. They ruled that separate but equal was okay. Only one judge felt differently. Judge J. Waties Waring, a white man, wrote an opinion in which he called segregation "evil." One white man's opinion was not enough to change history, but it gave the NAACP hope.

Marshall had expected this decision. He appealed the case to the U.S. Supreme Court. But the case was not heard for almost two years.

Meanwhile, Barbara Rose Johns, a high school junior in Farmville, Virginia, took matters into her own hands. Moton

High School held twice as many students as it was designed to hold. Its teachers were paid less than the lowest-paid white teacher in all of Prince Edward County. It had no cafeteria and no gym. The students complained, saying they needed more space. The county's answer was shacks made of tar paper and wood. Although parents and teachers complained, the county refused their request for a new school.

Barbara Rose Johns watched for months as the school board turned down requests from parents, teachers, and students. She decided it was time to take matters into her own hands. She planned a student strike.

As months went by, Barbara Rose Johns knew she had to take action. The first thing she did was have someone phone the school principal and tell him there were two students skipping school, heading for the Greyhound bus terminal. When the principal went to the terminal to pick up the students, Barbara forged his signature on notes to get the teachers to bring their students to a special assembly. After the students and the teachers had arrived at the assembly, Johns told the teachers what she had to say to the students was a surprise that she wanted to keep secret for the time being. She asked the teachers to leave and then told the students of Moton High the truth about her plan. She wanted them to go on strike.

What brought the students of Moton High together was the size of the town jail. There was no way, Johns told them, that all 450 of them could fit into the jail. The town would have to listen to them. When she finished, the students burst into cheers.

Despite the principal's plea for no strike, the students drew up a list of their demands. The next day, the classrooms were empty at Moton High.

On the third day of the strike, the students met with men from the NAACP. They were told that the NAACP would only represent them if their parents agreed to the terms—not to settle for separate but equal public facilities, but to demand desegregation of schools in Virginia. The students and parents agreed. The NAACP took the state of Virginia to court.

In 1953, a federal district court ruled against the NAACP in the *Moton High School* case. Once again, the NAACP appealed to the Supreme Court.

Meanwhile, Barbara Johns went to live with her uncle in Montgomery, Alabama, to avoid any violence from angry whites. Vernon Johns was the pastor of the Dexter Avenue Baptist Church. He was very involved in fighting against the poor treatment of local blacks on buses. Only a few years later, Thurgood Marshall and the NAACP would be fighting that battle as well.

11 THE CASE THAT CHANGED HISTORY

> *Any test the school wishes to give for one reason or another to separate children is okay with me except one—the racial test. That's all it comes down to. Not the racial test.*
>
> **THURGOOD MARSHALL**

Good Quote

While Barbara Johns was convincing the students of Moton High to strike, Thurgood Marshall and the other NAACP lawyers were setting their sights on Topeka, Kansas. Seven-year-old Linda Brown was attracting a lot of attention. Her father, Rev. Oliver Brown, had contacted the NAACP in 1950. He was fed up. He didn't think it was fair for his young daughter to cross dangerous train tracks and wait for a rickety old bus to go to school. It was especially unfair since there was a perfectly good school much closer to their home—a perfectly good all-white school.

The NAACP argued the case and lost. It was no surprise to anyone. Separate but equal. Separate but equal. That was the echo of the lower courts. The NAACP asked the U.S. Supreme Court to hear the case. But as with all the cases dealing with segregation at the elementary school level, the Court wasn't ready to decide on the constitutionality of the issue.

In June 1952, the Supreme Court announced that it would hear the case involving Linda Brown. The case was to be called *Brown* v. *The Board of Education of Topeka*. It would be a case about the constitutionality of the separate but equal law. It would include the case of Harry Briggs of Clarendon County. The NAACP prepared for the hearing. Then, on October 8, the Court postponed the case. They had decided to also include the case involving Barbara Rose Johns.

Ten days before the hearing began, Thurgood Marshall went to Washington. Although the NAACP had been preparing for all three cases, hoping that they would eventually be heard by the Supreme Court, Marshall still had a lot of work ahead of him. He stayed at the Statler Hotel, and day and night people came and went. They came to argue with him, hoping to bring up points he may not have thought of. They tried to guess what the Supreme Court needed to hear to overturn the *Plessy* decision. Of the 15 cases he had argued in front of the Supreme Court so far, Marshall had lost only 2. This was the most important case he would ever argue. Marshall never lost sight of the importance of the issue. He was not concerned with overwhelming all nine justices with his brilliance. All he wanted was for school segregation to become illegal. All he needed was five justices to agree.

The courtroom was packed on December 9, 1952. Marshall was up against John W. Davis, a lawyer who had argued more than 250 cases in front of the Supreme Court. He was 81 years old, a former solicitor general who had turned down a nomination to the Supreme Court in 1922, and one of the best lawyers in the United States. Marshall had his work cut out for him.

Marshall and Davis argued the case for three days. In a speech remembered by all who were there, Marshall pleaded the injustices of racism.

"I got the feeling," Marshall said,

[from what has been said here] that when you put a white child in a school with a whole lot of colored children, the children would fall apart or something. Everybody knows that is not true. Those same kids in Virginia and South Carolina—and I have seen them do it—they play in the streets together, they play on their farms together, they go down the road together, they separate to go to school, they come out of school and play ball together. They have to be separated in school....Why of all the [different kinds] of groups in this country [do] you have to single out the Negroes and give them this separate treatment? It can't be because of slavery in the past, because there are very few groups in this country that haven't had slavery some place in the history of their groups. It can't be color, because there are Negroes as white as drifted snow, with blue eyes, and they are just as segregated as the colored men. The only thing it can be is a [deep] determination that the people who were formerly in slavery, regardless of anything else, shall be kept as near that stage as possible. And now is the time...that this court should make it clear that that is not what our Constitution stands for.

The Supreme Court listened carefully for three days to arguments presented by each lawyer. At the end, there was no clear winner. Even the Court didn't feel it could make a decision this important based only on what it had heard. The justices gave both sides a list of questions concerning the 14th Amendment to the U.S. Constitution. Both sides were instructed to be prepared to answer the questions when the Court was ready to listen. Then the Court was silent.

Nine months later, the chief justice of the Supreme Court, Frederick M. Vinson, died of a heart attack. His death was completely unexpected, and for a month there was no chief justice. When President Dwight D. Eisenhower finally appointed a new chief justice, it was Earl Warren. No one knew for sure how the new chief justice would vote on the issue of separate but equal.

One year after the case had first been argued, the Court was ready to hear the answers to the questions it had asked. In December 1953, Marshall and Davis argued again. It was impossible to tell how the new chief justice felt about the issue. He was silent throughout most of the trial, watching and taking notes. The Court did not hand down a decision until five months later.

On Monday, May 17, 1954, the U.S. Supreme Court handed down a decision that changed history. Fifty-eight years after the same Court had made segregation legal in *Plessy* v. *Ferguson*, Chief Justice Earl Warren asked the question: "Does segregation of children in public schools solely on the basis of race, even though [everything] may be equal, [rob] the children... of equal educational opportunities?"

A courtroom full of people waited anxiously for the answer. "We believe that it does," answered Warren. "We conclude that in the field of public education... 'separate but equal' has no place."

This decision shocked many people. It had finally happened. The Supreme Court had overturned its own decision because it was unfair. Segregation in schools was now against the law! It had been a long fight for Marshall and the other lawyers of the NAACP. Charles Houston would have been proud. Nearly 25 years later, Marshall still remembered how Houston had affected them all. "A large number of people never heard of Charles Houston," he said. "[But] when Brown against the Board of Education was being argued in the Supreme Court... there were some two dozen lawyers on the side of the Negroes fighting for their schools.... Of those lawyers, only two hadn't been touched by Charlie Houston.... That man was the engineer of all of it." Charles Houston may have engineered it. But Thurgood Marshall argued the blacks of the United States into equality. All that remained was for the whites of the United States to accept the law.

BLACK MONDAY

> ❝ *The...soil...draws no color line. The sun draws no color line. The rain draws no color line.* ❞
>
> **BOOKER T. WASHINGTON**

Thurgood Marshall was "so happy, [he] was numb." But not everyone was as pleased with the *Brown* v. *Board of Education* decision. Many people in the northern states celebrated. But in the South where racial hatred ran deep, the day of the decision became known as Black Monday. The governor of South Carolina said he would make every school in the state a private school rather than desegregate. In Mississippi, a school superintendent said the decision didn't bother him at all because "...we're not going to [follow] it in our county. It will be 'to Hell with the Supreme Court down here.'"

There still remained the question of how to integrate the schools. The Supreme Court gave the NAACP Legal Defense Fund five months to come up with a plan, and its recommendations were handed in within the given time period. But the Court did not make its decision on how to integrate for eight months. During this waiting period, Marshall spent a lot of time at home. Buster was sick.

Thurgood had been so wrapped up in the *Brown* case that the doctor had waited to tell him what was wrong with Buster. When Marshall found out, he was horrified. His wife had lung cancer. There was nothing anyone could do. In February 1955, Vivian (Buster) Marshall died.

Buster and Thurgood had no children, and his wife's death left him lonely and sad. Thurgood buried his grief in his work. He knew it would be a long time before he stopped mourning the death of the woman he had loved for 26 years.

There was plenty to keep Thurgood busy in the days after Buster's death. On May 31, 1955, the Supreme Court handed down their final decision on the *Brown* v. *Board of Education of Topeka* case. It was a surprising decision to many people. Instead of ruling when the entire country should end school segregation, the Court left the matter up to each state to decide. Lower courts would be responsible for seeing that desegregation began "with all deliberate speed." That sentence meant a lot of work for the NAACP. "With all deliberate speed" meant that many states would try to avoid desegregation. And that meant the NAACP was still going to have to fight it out in court. When someone told Thurgood Marshall that the state of Georgia would fight the decision in all of its 159 counties, Marshall said that was fine, he'd take every one of them to court.

Reaction to the Supreme Court decision was the most violent in the Deep South. In Mississippi, gangs of whites burned down the homes and churches of blacks. There were more lynchings than ever. But there was something different about the people who were being murdered. In the past, a black would

Emmett Till, the 14-year-old boy who was murdered for the "crime" of speaking to a white woman.

be killed for stealing or for talking to a white. Now the people who were being killed were those trying to convince southern blacks to try to stand up for their rights—rights that the Supreme Court of the country had said were theirs by law. The people being killed were both black and white. Then, in August 1955, the entire country was forced to look at a brutal murder.

Emmett Till was a fun-loving black boy from Chicago visiting relatives in Mississippi. Emmett was fond of pulling pranks.

On a Wednesday evening in August 1955 he pulled a prank that would have made no difference in the life of a white boy. But being a black in Mississippi was a different matter.

Emmett and his friends were joking around outside a local country store called Bryant's Grocery and Meat Market. Emmett showed them a picture of a friend from Chicago, a white girl. He bragged about how she was "his girl," all in harmless fun. "Hey," said one of his friends, "there's a [white] girl in that store there. I bet you won't go in there and talk to her." Taking the dare, Emmett walked into the store and bought some candy. On his way out, he made his move. "Bye, Baby," he said to the white woman, whose name was Carolyn Bryant. The boys then jumped in their car and drove off. They told this great story of daring to all their friends for the next few days.

According to accounts, this is what happened next. When Carolyn Bryant's husband heard that a black kid had said "Bye, Baby" to his wife, he called his brother-in-law. They kidnapped Emmett Till and drove him to a river. There they made him carry a 75-pound cotton-gin fan from the back of the truck to the river bank. Then they made him strip. Then they shot him in the head. When Emmett Till's body was found three days later, the barbed wire holding the cotton-gin fan to his back had become snagged on a root of a tree in the river. There was a bullet in his head, his forehead was crushed, and one eye was gouged out. "What else could we do," the brother-in-law later told a white journalist. "He was hopeless. I'm no bully; I never hurt a nigger in my life. I like niggers in their place. I know how to work 'em. But I just decided it was time a few people got put on notice." An all-white jury found the accused killers not guilty.

Thirty-three years after a 14-year-old boy named Thurgood Marshall hit a white man and lived, another 14-year-old boy didn't have Thurgood's luck. Thirty-three years later, the United States of America hadn't changed that much.

Emmett Till's death had a powerful effect on the nation. His body was so badly mangled that the only way he could be identified was by a ring he always wore. The local sheriff wanted to bury the body immediately, but Emmett's mother, Mamie Bradley, wanted the body shipped back to her in Chicago. The body arrived in a closed casket, with a notice attached that said it was not to be opened.

Mamie Bradley opened the casket. And she kept it opened through the funeral. "Have you ever sent a loved son on vacation and had him returned to you in a pine box, so horribly battered and water-logged that someone needs to tell you this sickening sight is your son—lynched?" she asked reporters later. But as grief stricken as she was, Mamie Bradley was determined to have "the world see what they did to my boy." She waited four days to bury the body, so everyone who wanted to could view the corpse. On the first day the casket was open, about 2,000 people came to the church. But the photo *Jet* magazine published of Emmett Till's corpse shocked a nation.

In Montgomery, Alabama, where Barbara Rose Johns had gone to live, a newspaper, the *Montgomery Advertiser*, picked up the story of Emmett Till. Three months later, a woman named Rosa Parks moved the eyes of the country from Mississippi to Montgomery.

On December 1, 1955, Rosa Parks, a 42-year-old black woman, boarded a bus in Montgomery, Alabama, and sat down. She sat in the first row of the middle section of seats. In Montgomery, a black was allowed to sit in these seats, as long as a white wasn't left standing. At the next stop, more whites boarded the bus, and most of them sat down. There weren't enough seats for all of them, and a white man was left standing. What happened next set off a string of events that would change the United States forever.

The bus driver told Rosa Parks and the three other blacks to move. When they didn't, he threatened them: "Y'all better make it light on yourself and let me have those seats," he said. The three other blacks rose immediately. Rosa Parks stayed seated.

"When he saw me still sitting," Parks remembered, "he asked if I was going to stand up, and I said, 'No, I'm not.' And he said, 'Well, if you don't stand up, I'm going to have to call the police and have you arrested.' I said, 'You may do that.'"

Rosa Parks was taken to jail and booked for breaking the bus segregation laws of Montgomery. When she got thirsty, she was denied a drink of water. The water fountain at the police station was for whites only.

News of Parks's arrest soon reached the ears of E. D. Nixon. Nixon had been the head of the Montgomery chapter of the NAACP when Rosa Parks was its secretary. When Nixon called the jail to find out why Parks had been arrested, no one would talk to him. Finally he had Clifford Durr, a white lawyer, call and discover the reason. Then Nixon raised the money and bailed Rosa Parks out. He told her that he wanted to make her case a cause in the fight against racism. He thought the time had come to attack bus segregation in Montgomery.

At five o'clock the next morning, E. D. Nixon began a series of calls to contact the ministers and black leaders in Montgomery. Among them was a new minister, a Rev. Martin Luther King, Jr. A meeting was called for that night. They would discuss what could be done about Rosa Parks's arrest.

Meanwhile, a woman named Jo Ann Robinson had met with a group of women and convinced them that now was the time for action. When an organized group refuses to do something, it is called a *boycott*. Jo Ann Robinson wanted to boycott Montgomery's buses.

By the time the ministers and black leaders met on Friday night, 35,000 fliers had been passed out to the blacks of Montgomery. Printed on a single sheet of paper, the fliers called for a complete boycotting of Montgomery's buses on Monday, December 5, 1955. "Another Negro woman has been arrested. . . . Don't ride the buses to work, to town, to school, or anywhere. . ." pleaded the fliers. While many blacks agreed immediately to the boycott, others were scared. Many walked out of the meeting in frustration or anger. Boycotting the buses could get a lot of blacks fired from their jobs. They would be hassled and threatened by whites on the streets and possibly not allowed to shop in local stores. They knew it was a risk people were going to have to take if they wanted the boycott to be successful. If everyone didn't go along with it, the boycott wouldn't work.

When the meeting was over, E. D. Nixon called a white reporter for the *Montgomery Advertiser* and told him he had a great story for him. The story on the front page of the paper Sunday morning spread the word to any blacks who may have missed the fliers. The word was out to everyone now. Including the police. They arranged to have cops trailing each bus.

Monday morning was chilly—a cold morning to be walking to work. The sign at a main downtown bus stop read People Don't Ride the Buses Today. Don't Ride It for Freedom. The 18 black-owned taxi companies in Montgomery had all agreed to provide transportation for the same amount as it would cost on the bus—10¢ a ride. Everything was ready. It was only five-thirty in the morning. The first bus had not yet arrived.

When the first bus did arrive, no one got on. As the sun rose slowly in the sky, the streets became crowded with people on their way to work. Bus after bus stopped at their regular stops and moved on empty, leaving a trail of blacks walking in its path. Taxis were packed with blacks on their way to work. Groups of blacks walked and rode bicycles; one person even rode a mule. Thousands of blacks walked proudly to work.

That morning, Rosa Parks was found guilty as charged. She was ordered to pay a $10 fine and $4 in court costs. The surprise came when she tried to leave the courtroom. Almost 500 blacks crowded the halls and corridors of the courthouse. Not only was the boycott successful, the blacks of Montgomery had united. They now had a cause.

That afternoon, the Montgomery Improvement Association

(MIA) was formed. It was a group of ministers and black leaders who wanted to make sure that this wasn't just a one-day boycott with no effect. They wanted to kick Jim Crow off the buses. The Reverend Martin Luther King, Jr., was elected the leader of the MIA. That night, he made the first of many speeches. A thousand people crowded into the church. Four thousand more stood outside the door. "There comes a time," he said, "when people get tired . . . of being kicked about. . . ." The crowd roared their support of this new minister. When they quieted down, he told them of his message of peace. It was the message of one of King's idols, Mohandas Gandhi. In India, Gandhi had led his people to freedom with words of peace and protests of nonviolence. King wanted Montgomery's blacks to do the same. "In spite of the mistreatment we have [met with] we must not be bitter and end up by hating our white brothers," King said. He told the people to protest without violence. "If we protest courageously, and yet with dignity and . . . love," he said, "when the history books are written in the future, somebody will have to say, 'there lived a race of people, of black people . . . who had the courage to stand up for their rights.'" Then King and the others drew up a list of demands to bring to the owners of the bus companies and to the mayor of Montgomery.

Their demands were rejected. So the bus boycott continued. It lasted through December and on into March. King and other black leaders received hate mail, hate phone calls, and death threats. But King continued to preach peace and nonviolence to the people of Montgomery. He knew that the next step in this protest had to be handled in the courts. Thurgood Marshall and the NAACP had once again taken the issue of segregation to the U.S. Supreme Court. If they could get the Court to declare bus segregation unconstitutional, it would be another great step toward total equality for blacks.

Almost a year after Rosa Parks refused to give up her seat, the Supreme Court ruled that Jim Crow bus laws were unconstitu-

Ralph Abernathy (front left) and Martin Luther King, Jr.
(second row left), ride a Montgomery bus.

tional. The boycott was over. On December 21, 1956, the blacks
of Montgomery, Alabama, boarded the buses and sat down
wherever they pleased. It was a wonderful victory for the people of Montgomery, Alabama. Indeed, all over the country,
blacks were celebrating another victory in the fight against racism. Thurgood Marshall had little time to rejoice. He was
dealing with racism of a very violent nature.

BLOOD IN THE STREETS

> ❝ We ain't what we ought to be and we ain't what we want to be and we ain't what we're going to be. But thank God we ain't what we was. ❞
>
> MARTIN LUTHER KING, JR., quoting an old black slave

As Thurgood Marshall had expected, most of the southern states were doing everything they could to keep black children out of their all-white schools. Most of his time was spent trying to see that school systems obeyed the 1954 law to desegregate. While Marshall and the NAACP were waiting for the bus desegregation issue to reach the U.S. Supreme Court, Marshall was in the South, fighting for the rights of blacks who wanted nothing more than a good education.

Authurine J. Lucy had been trying to enroll in the University of Alabama since September 1952. She had been turned away

Violence Against African Americans

White violence against African Americans was common in the United States, even after slavery ended. Groups of whites sometimes took African Americans from their homes to beat, shoot, or lynch them. The home was no place for protection against such violence. In fact, the home could be—and often was—burned down.

It was acceptable in many places for whites to treat blacks badly. This treatment would have been a crime if the black victim had been white. But many local white law officers permitted these activities. The national government stood by without doing much of anything until the civil rights movement of the 1950s and 1960s began to bring about the needed changes.

Many black people's homes or churches, like this one, were torched or bombed by white bigots.

The bodies of four African Americans wait to be buried.
These four men were lynched.

The body of an African American is burned by a
lynch mob in Omaha, Nebraska, in 1919.

from the school because she was black. Marshall and the NAACP took the case to court. Judge Grooms of the District Court for the Northern District of Alabama told the University of Alabama to admit Lucy and any other black students who applied. The university appealed the case and won. Marshall took the case to the U.S. Supreme Court. The Court demanded that Lucy be admitted to the University of Alabama.

On February 6, 1956, with Thurgood Marshall at her side, Authurine Lucy went to college. Some of the students at the university and citizens of the town had planned a surprise for Lucy. As she walked proudly toward her class, they threw rocks and eggs at her. The next day, the school told Lucy she couldn't come back. It was for her own safety, they said, and for the safety of the other students and teachers.

Marshall was furious. He appeared before the district court in Birmingham, Alabama, and argued that his client was being punished for doing something that was within her legal right to do. On February 29, Judge Grooms ordered the University of Alabama to let Lucy return to school. Immediately after this, the trustees of the university kicked Authurine Lucy out of school permanently. They said it was because of harmful comments she and her lawyer had made during the court hearing.

Marshall was ready to continue arguing the case in court. But Lucy was in need of rest and medical attention. She flew to New York and did not attempt to return to the University of Alabama. On April 22 of that year, she was married in Dallas.

All over the South, schools were refusing to integrate. Marshall was determined to see it happen. He took case after case to court. The situation finally exploded in September 1957 in the city of Little Rock, Arkansas.

The school board of Little Rock did not want to integrate its schools. But when a federal court ordered Central High School to admit nine black students, the board had no choice. The Supreme Court had said segregation was illegal. So Central High had to desegregate. It was the law.

Towns such as this were not uncommon in the 1950s in their fight against integration and civil rights.

The governor of Arkansas, Orval Faubus, didn't agree with the law. The night before the new school session opened, he went on statewide television, announcing that he was going to surround the school with National Guardsmen. He said, "Blood will run in the streets if Negro pupils should attempt to enter Central High School." The case brought nationwide attention to the town. The students became known as the Little Rock Nine.

The next day 250 National Guardsmen surrounded Central High. The students had agreed the night before to go to school as a group. But one student, 15-year-old Elizabeth Eckford, did not have a phone and wasn't told about the plan. She arrived at Central High that morning completely alone and was met by an army of soldiers and an angry mob of whites. No one would let her get through to the school, not even the guards. When the mob turned nasty, the soldiers did not make a move to protect her.

Four of the Little Rock Nine are turned away from Central High School by National Guard troops.

Elizabeth fled the angry mob and tried to wait at a nearby bus stop. The crowd followed her, calling out to each other to drag her to a nearby tree and lynch her. A white woman finally helped young Elizabeth escape. When the eight other students arrived at Central High, they were turned away by the National Guard.

Thurgood Marshall was in Little Rock to see that the students' legal rights were protected. When asked if he saw the situation as a fight between the government of a state and the government of the United States, Marshall replied, "I don't think there's any doubt about that." The Supreme Court had created the problem when it left the issue of desegregation to the individual states. Now only the president of the United States could help. And Marshall and the other members of the NAACP Legal Defense Fund were disappointed in President Eisenhower. He was in a position to send enough federal troops down to protect the Little Rock Nine. Instead, he did nothing but have a conversation with Governor Faubus.

On Monday morning, September 23, the Little Rock Nine went to school. By noon that day, more than 1,000 angry whites surrounded the school. They yelled horrible words at the black students and called for the white students to leave the school. The police chief was afraid a riot would break out, so the Little Rock Nine were sent home.

The next morning the same thing happened. This time, President Eisenhower sent in federal troops. Three hundred and fifty paratroopers surrounded Central High School. They had guns and bayonets. The Little Rock Nine were escorted into the school. Once inside, each was assigned a bodyguard. The white students were far more accepting than their parents had been. One of the Little Rock Nine, Minniejean Brown, was invited to join the glee club. Some of the others were invited to eat lunch with the white students.

For a while, everything was calm at Central High School. But slowly, racial hatred crept back into the classrooms. At first, it was name-calling and water guns. It was hard to take, but the Little Rock Nine had put up with worse. Then one day, Minniejean Brown couldn't take it any longer. A group of white students had been following her around for weeks, chanting "nigger, nigger, nigger." In the lunch line at school one day, without saying a word, she picked up her chili and dumped it on the head of the white kid behind her. She was suspended from school. In February, a girl called her a "nigger bitch." Minniejean called the girl "white trash." This time, Minniejean Brown was expelled from school.

Now only eight students remained. And at the end of the school year, Ernest Green became the first black to graduate from Central High School. Then Governor Faubus was reelected.

In February 1958, at about the same time that Minniejean Brown was expelled from school, Central High asked a district court to postpone complete desegregation of the school for two and a half years. The school board said the reason for this request was that there was tension and unrest among the students and teachers, and the court agreed. Thurgood Marshall appealed the case. Eventually, the Supreme Court held a special session in August to hear the appeal. Marshall argued that "even if it [can] be claimed that tension will result which will disturb the education process, this is [better than] the complete breakdown of education which will [happen if we teach children] that courts of law will bow to violence." The 1958–59 school year had already started at Central High. The Supreme Court ruled that the black students there could stay in school and that complete desegregation should begin immediately.

Governor Faubus's answer to the Court was to close down all the schools in Little Rock. Then private schools took the white students from the public schools. A public opinion poll taken that year showed that Americans found Governor Faubus one of the 10 most admired men in the United States.

Little Rock's schools remained closed throughout 1958. Many students, both black and white, did not go to school at all that year. In 1959, the Supreme Court ruled that the closing of the schools was unconstitutional. The high schools were reopened in August 1959. At last, maybe the nation's schools would truly be integrated.

Thurgood Marshall had said the NAACP would take a case to court every time a black student was turned away from a school. He kept his word. If the NAACP heard about the case, it went to court. It was an overwhelming amount of work, but Marshall tried to be anywhere he was needed. Blacks and whites alike called him "Mr. Civil Rights."

Marshall gained tremendous respect for the students and local NAACP leaders he met in the South. "There isn't a threat known to men that they do not receive," he said. "They're never out from under pressure. I don't think I could take it for a week. The possibility of violent death for them and their families is something they've learned to live with like a man learns to sleep with a sore arm."

The subject of families was on Marshall's mind a lot these days. As busy as he was, he missed the warmth and security of a home. In 1955, he married again. The woman's name was Cecilia Suyat. "Hawaiian-born Cissy" had been Marshall's secretary at the NAACP. She decided to quit her job soon after they married to raise a family. Thurgood, Jr., was born in 1956 and John in 1958. Now Marshall spent as many nights at home as he could, playing with his children.

All over the country, African Americans were rising up in protest of the way they were treated. They had won the battle over school desegregation. And a war had been won on bus desegregation. But much of the nation was still divided into black and white. The next challenge was the desegregation of restaurants and cafeterias.

In February 1960, a few black students walked into a restaurant in Greensboro, North Carolina. They sat down at the all-white lunch counter and waited to be served. The waiter refused to serve them. The students sat and waited. They waited all day. But they were never served. So they came back the next day and waited again. Soon they were joined by other black students. Then, by white students who refused to eat unless everyone was served. In a very short time, there were sit-ins at lunch counters throughout the South. Martin Luther King, Jr., even joined a sit-in at a lunch counter in Atlanta, Georgia.

As head of the NAACP's Legal Defense Fund, Marshall was not sure if he should support the student sit-ins. He and many other members of the NAACP believed that change could and should be gained through the courts. Marshall was aware that bus boycotts and student sit-ins raised basic legal questions that he could further explore in court. After all, the Montgomery bus boycott had paved the way for Marshall to argue bus desegregation in front of the U.S. Supreme Court. Still, Marshall wasn't sure what to do about the sit-ins. What if large groups of

Three college students try to get service during a sit-in at a lunch counter in Greensboro, North Carolina.

people involved in sit-ins or demonstrations became violent? Weren't these issues best saved for the courtroom?

Marshall called a meeting of 60 civil rights lawyers to discuss this issue. They met at his old school, Howard University. After listening carefully to both sides of the issue, Marshall made a decision. On March 20, 1960, he announced that $40,000 had been set aside to defend those who peacefully took part in sit-ins and other demonstrations. "If a dime store is open to the public, anyone who enters [should get] the same service anyone else gets," he said. "The right of protest is part of our tradition. It goes back to tea dumped in Boston Harbor. They have a right to say they want their rights. As long as they act lawfully, we will support them."

Marshall was working harder than ever. He traveled 50,000 miles a year. He handled 500 to 600 cases that involved 2,000 to 3,000 people. Marshall was such a highly respected lawyer that he was offered a $50,000-a-year job. That was an incredible amount of money then. But he refused to leave the NAACP.

Meanwhile the sit-ins and protests continued. There was name-calling, and there was violence. Many of the students were arrested. By October 1960, sit-ins had taken place in 112 cities throughout the South. Many of the sit-ins were still going on.

Those involved in the civil rights movement had reason to be hopeful. In the past few years, the U.S. Supreme Court had slowly ruled that segregation was illegal. In December 1960, the Court ordered those bus stations and terminals that served people from more than one state to integrate. Now there was one more law making segregation illegal. There was also a new president.

In 1960, there was a presidential election. For the first time, enough African Americans voted to help elect a president. His name was John F. Kennedy. To many, he was the hope of a nation. While running for office, he had made it clear that he was on the side of civil rights. When Martin Luther King, Jr., was arrested unfairly at a sit-in, Kennedy helped to free him from jail. In one of his campaign speeches he said, "It is in the American tradition to stand up for one's rights—even if the new way to stand up for one's rights is to sit down."

In 1961, President Kennedy named a new federal judge: Thurgood Marshall. Kennedy appointed Marshall as a judge on the U.S. Court of Appeals for the Second Circuit. Marshall wasn't sure whether he should take the job or not. "I had to fight it out with myself," he said. "But by then I had built up a staff—a good staff . . . [at the NAACP]. And when one has the opportunity to serve his government, he should think twice before passing it up." Marshall took the job.

SITTING DOWN FOR FREEDOM

❝ Race has no place in private place or law. ❞

PRESIDENT JOHN F. KENNEDY

The NAACP hated to lose Marshall. But it knew a judgeship was an important move for him. Now he would be on the deciding end of cases other lawyers argued in court. In the four years he spent on the bench, Marshall wrote almost one hundred opinions. Not one of his decisions was reversed when a lawyer appealed a case to the U.S. Supreme Court.

It was considered an honor to be appointed to the court on which Marshall now served. He was, however, a junior member of the court and was not assigned the most difficult cases. As a result, Marshall did not deal with the kinds of cases he had been so involved with as head of the NAACP Legal Defense Fund. Others had rather strong opinions about Marshall's time on the U.S. Court of Appeals. A journalist for *The New York Times Magazine* called Marshall's lack of knowledge about tax law embarrassing. Journalist James J. Kilpatrick, who specialized in judicial matters, wrote in the conservative *National Review* magazine, "Marshall was a dull judge in the four terms he served on the Second Circuit....I recently spent some hours in the Supreme Court Library...and did not find a quotable phrase or an original thought." Kilpatrick also admitted that it would be hard for even the best judge in the world to "shine in most of the cases that were assigned to Marshall for opinions."

Marshall was busy on the court, but he always kept an eye on the sit-ins, boycotts, and other protest movements rising up around the country. These movements were paving the way for more and more legal action to be taken by the NAACP.

Martin Luther King, Jr., had a rather large following by this time. More than once King told his followers to support the efforts that Marshall had begun. "We must continue our struggle in the courts," said King. "Above all, we must continue to support the NAACP. Our major victories have come through the work of this organization." Marshall was now Judge Marshall and unable to participate in the workings of the NAACP. But many others were carrying on in his footsteps, continuing to try to change the way the nation treated African Americans.

For the first few years that Thurgood Marshall sat on the U.S. Court of Appeals, the Freedom Riders rode across the United States. In May 1961, groups of people, black and white, began riding interstate buses through the South in the name of freedom. They rode with blacks in front and whites in the back of the buses. They rode that way as a protest against racial segregation. Almost everywhere they went, they met with much name-calling and violence. The farther south they rode, the worse the violence became. But nowhere was it worse for them than in Alabama.

James Peck was one of the injured Freedom Riders who were firebombed outside Birmingham.

On May 14, Mother's Day, buses filled with Freedom Riders were on their way into Anniston, Alabama, when the threats became a terrible truth. One bus broke down on the highway and was attacked by a white mob armed with clubs. The mob threw a firebomb into the bus and tried to hold the doors closed while it burned. The Freedom Riders aboard fled for their lives in panic, climbing out windows as the crowd battered them. Many had to be taken to hospitals.

Another bus continued into the town. When it reached the terminal there, more whites surrounded it and savagely beat the passengers. Among the victims was Walter Bergman, a 63-year-old sociology professor who was riding with his wife. The citizens of Anniston beat him so brutally that he suffered permanent brain damage and was paralyzed for life.

The FBI had known in advance that this would happen. But they did nothing, and the local police stayed away. "When you

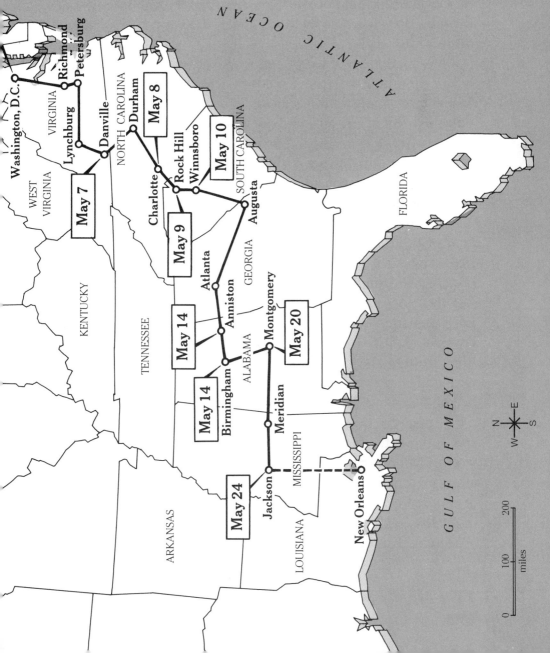

THE ROUTE OF THE FREEDOM RIDERS 1961

ATLANTIC OCEAN

GULF OF MEXICO

Washington, D.C.

May 7

Richmond

Petersburg

Lynchburg

Danville

Durham — May 8

May 10

Winnsboro

Rock Hill

Charlotte

May 9

Augusta

Atlanta

May 14 — Anniston

May 14 — Birmingham

Montgomery — May 20

Meridian

May 24 — Jackson

New Orleans

WEST VIRGINIA

VIRGINIA

NORTH CAROLINA

SOUTH CAROLINA

KENTUCKY

TENNESSEE

GEORGIA

ALABAMA

MISSISSIPPI

ARKANSAS

LOUISIANA

FLORIDA

0   100   200
miles

N
W   E
S

go somewhere looking for trouble, you usually find it," said Alabama's governor, John Patterson.

The same "trouble" followed the buses to Birmingham. Martin Luther King, Jr., once called Birmingham the most segregated city in the country. After the Anniston attacks, President Kennedy called Governor Wallace and asked for his promise to protect the Freedom Riders from the mobs there. It was a promise the governor did not keep. Freedom Riders kept traveling to Birmingham, where they were attacked by angry crowds or thrown into jail.

The situation grew worse and worse over the next few days. From Birmingham, the Freedom Riders took the bus to Montgomery, only 90 miles away. They were met with a cry of "kill the niggers." Bricks and sticks were thrown at them, followed by more beatings and arrests. On May 20, after Governor Wallace refused to act against the mobs, President Kennedy sent 400 U.S. marshals to Montgomery to keep the peace.

Two years later, in May 1963, Martin Luther King, Jr., led a march through the streets of Birmingham. It was a different kind of protest this time. In the past, many blacks had been fired from their jobs or beaten for participating in marches or protests. So King looked for a group of protesters who wouldn't lose their jobs and whom no one would want to beat or arrest. He led a march of children, some as young as six years old, on a crusade against segregation. One thousand of them followed him through the streets of Birmingham. But he had been wrong. The police used school buses to take the children to jail.

The following day, 1,000 more children marched with King. This time, the police attacked them with German shepherds and sprayed them with water from fire hoses. Although less violent than other protests, this demonstration drew the eyes of a horrified nation on Birmingham. The televised news footage of children being mauled by police dogs and blasted with water disgusted many people.

More and more people joined the Birmingham marches for

freedom. By May 6, the city jails were filled with 2,000 people. Four thousand more were marching in the streets. With nowhere else to put the protesters and an entire country waiting to see what they would do, the white police officers of Birmingham finally disobeyed orders and walked away from the protesters. The marchers had made headway in kicking Jim Crow out of Birmingham, Alabama. Victory was at last in sight!

Thurgood Marshall was more concerned with what was going on in Washington than in Birmingham. It looked as if President Kennedy was not going to sign the new civil rights bill. Although he believed in it, the president's advisers were telling him that he would anger too many of his southern supporters if he signed the bill. Even if Marshall had still been with the NAACP, there was little that he or any lawyer could do. It was going to take a lot of pressure from a lot of people to convince the president to sign the bill. Marshall and the NAACP wanted to join forces with such leaders as Martin Luther King, Jr., and others. Under the direction of A. Philip Randolph, a March on Washington, D.C., was organized. King lent his support by stepping in as a featured speaker.

On August 28, 1963, 250,000 people gathered in Washington, D.C. They came by car and by bus. They came by plane and by train. Some even walked. They came to Washington from all different walks of life. Men and women, black and white, gathered at the foot of Abraham Lincoln's statue to hear a speech that has gone down in history as one of the greatest speeches of all time. "I have a dream," began Dr. Martin Luther King, Jr.

> I have a dream that one day on the red hills of Georgia, the sons of former slaves and the sons of former slave owners will be able to sit down at the table of brotherhood. . . . I have a dream that my four little children will one day live in a nation where they will not be judged by the color of their skin, but by the content of their character. . . . Let

From the Lincoln Memorial, a view of the 1963 March on Washington, a protest against racial inequality.

Freedom Ring from the mighty mountains of New York.... Let Freedom Ring from every hill and molehill in Mississippi... until one day... all of God's children... will be able to join hands and sing in the words of the old Negro spiritual, "Free at last! Free at last! Thank God Almighty, we are free at last!"

The March on Washington united much of the country in its pursuit of civil rights. The barriers of segregation were breaking down faster and faster every day. But 18 days after the march, the eyes of the country were once again on Birmingham, Alabama, where dynamite exploded in a church, killing four children. They were at a Bible class when the church exploded. On the same day, the Birmingham police killed a young black man, and a gang of whites attacked and killed a black man on a bicycle. In November of the same year, President John F. Kennedy was assassinated in Dallas, Texas.

Before he was killed, President Kennedy had submitted the civil rights bill to Congress. The bill outlawed all forms of racial discrimination.

On July 2, 1964, the bill became law. When the new president, President Johnson, signed the bill, he said: "Those who are equal before God shall now be equal in the polling booths, in the classrooms, the factories, and in the hotels, restaurants, movie theaters, and other places that provide services to the public." Segregation was finally illegal in all walks of life.

President Johnson signs the landmark and long overdue Civil Rights Act of 1964.

The Civil Rights Act did not put an end to discrimination and racism. A law cannot stop people from being racist. It can only stop them from illegal behavior. In many southern counties, blacks were not being allowed to register in order to vote. In Selma, Alabama, the situation was particularly bad. No blacks were being allowed to register to vote. They would wait in line for hours and then be told the office was closed. They would be asked inappropriate questions like: "Does your employer know you're here?" Sometimes one or two blacks were allowed to register before the office was closed. But it was always closed soon afterward.

A march was organized to protest this treatment of blacks. The march would start in Selma and end at the state capital of Montgomery four days later. The march began peacefully. Two by two, the protesters walked until they reached the Edmund Pettus Bridge. Suddenly there was violence everywhere. Police used tear gas, clubs, and buckshot to hold back the marchers. They let their horses trample on fallen protesters. The marchers retreated. But television stations had already interrupted their regular programs to show the world what was happening in Alabama. From that day on, Sunday, March 7, 1965, was known as Bloody Sunday.

Another march was scheduled. This time, protesters came to Selma from around the country. Overnight, more than 400 black and white ministers, rabbis, priests, and nuns flew to Selma, Alabama. They staged a short march. One of the white ministers, Rev. James Reeb of Boston, was attacked while leaving a restaurant in Selma. He was beaten so badly by four men that he died two days later.

President Johnson was shocked and outraged. He called Governor Wallace and laid down the law. The march would take place, and there would be no violence. To ensure this, Johnson sent 2,000 National Guardsmen, 100 FBI agents, and 100 federal marshals to Selma to protect the marchers. On March 15, 1965, he appeared on television to call for a national voting rights act. This act would protect the rights of all Americans to vote. "About this there can be no argument," he said. "Every American citizen must have an equal right to vote."

One week later, on March 21, 1965, four thousand people began the 50-mile march from Selma to Montgomery. They came from every walk of life. White nuns marched next to black children. Nobel Prize winners marched next to those who couldn't read. All around they were protected by the army. This march was different. There was more pride and less fear this time. They carried the American flag and sang as they marched. At night, they slept in tents that they pitched along the way. A team of volunteers brought them food and water. By the time they reached Montgomery, there were 25,000 marchers.

The protesters arrived in Montgomery on March 25. Martin Luther King, Jr., spoke to the people, and they sang together. Then King and seven others tried to present their demands to Governor Wallace. He refused to see them, so they gave the demands to his secretary and moved on. That night, a white woman who had marched was driving herself and the black boy who had carried the American flag back to Selma when she was shot in the face and killed by a Ku Klux Klansman in a passing car. There were still many battles to be fought.

As a result of the march from Selma to Montgomery, a new bill was passed in Congress. The Voting Rights Act of 1965 ordered federal examiners to protect the rights of all citizens to register and vote. The bill outlawed many of the tricks that had been used to stop blacks from voting, such as unfair reading tests and poll taxes that many blacks couldn't afford to pay. Immediately after the bill became law, blacks around the country registered to vote in record numbers. In only three years, the number of black voters in the South tripled to over 3 million.

Shortly after the Voting Rights Act was signed, the Watts section of Los Angeles, California, exploded in riots. The six-

PROTEST DEMONSTRATIONS IN THE SOUTH

Bus Boycott

Demonstrations

Freedom Ride Stop

March

Student Sit-ins

School Integration

★ State Capital

ATLANTIC OCEAN

GULF OF MEXICO

Washington, D.C.

VIRGINIA
★ Richmond

NORTH CAROLINA
★ Raleigh
Greensboro ●

SOUTH CAROLINA
★ Columbia

St. Augustine ●

FLORIDA

KENTUCKY
★ Frankfort

TENNESSEE
Knoxville ★
Nashville ●

GEORGIA
Atlanta ★
Albany ●
★ Tallahassee

ALABAMA
Anniston ●
Birmingham ●
Tuscaloosa ●
Selma ★ Montgomery
Mobile ●

MISSISSIPPI
Oxford ●
Meridian ●
★ Jackson

Memphis ●

ARKANSAS
★ Little Rock

LOUISIANA
★ Baton Rouge
New Orleans ●

N
W   E
S

0   100   200
miles

day riot in Watts was one of the worst riots in the history of the country. Thirty-four African Americans were killed. Six hundred people were injured. Forty-six million dollars worth of property was destroyed. There were race riots in cities across the country. People died and houses burned. But this time, it wasn't only at the hands of angry whites. A new wave of blacks were moving onto the civil rights scene—blacks who were frustrated and critical of King's message of nonviolence. They wanted to attack those who attacked them. They thought all the destruction would make the country pay more attention to them. Suddenly in a single act, the heights of respect that the civil rights movement had reached through peaceful protest had fallen away into a pit of hatred.

On April 4, 1968, Dr. Martin Luther King, Jr., was killed. A man of peace, he was shot on a balcony in Memphis, Tennessee. The nation was shocked. How could this have happened? The country mourned his death.

Thurgood Marshall was appointed solicitor general only two days before the riot in Watts broke out. The solicitor general is basically "Uncle Sam's attorney" in lawsuits brought by or against the federal government. Marshall was now a lawyer once again—the third-highest-ranking lawyer in the United States. In his new position, Marshall would decide which cases the government would appeal to the Supreme Court. As solicitor general, he would mostly be concerned with civil rights cases.

John F. Kennedy and Martin Luther King, Jr., had been murdered. Frustration and anger at their deaths spurred still more violence, as riots protesting the murders erupted across the country. But Thurgood Marshall was not violent. He continued to fight the battle against racism not with bricks but with words. His tool of peace was the U.S. Constitution. He believed, as he had always believed, that the courtroom was the place in which to change the world.

15 BUT WERE YOU IN SELMA WITH MARTIN LUTHER KING, JR.?

> **"** *It takes no courage to get in the back of a crowd and throw a rock.* **"**
>
> *Thurgood Marshall*

Although much of his new job involved arguing over tiny details of law, Marshall enjoyed being a lawyer again and won many of the civil rights cases he argued in front of the U.S. Supreme Court. In 1966, he won cases against the Ku Klux Klan in Georgia and Mississippi. In another case, Marshall argued that an unfair practice doesn't have to be mentioned in the 14th Amendment to be outlawed by it. It was another important victory for him.

In addition to the legal battles he continued to fight in the courtrooms, Marshall was called upon to make speeches about peace and civil rights at conferences and universities. He spoke to graduating college students and the members of the Supreme Court. On July 11, 1966, Marshall was former president Harry Truman's representative at a peace conference in Jerusalem.

There were those who were critical of the new solicitor general. They didn't like the fact that he lost 5 of the 19 cases he argued in front of the Supreme Court and was closely involved with several other cases that the government lost. But those who worked closely with him found him somewhere between good and excellent. Most important, President Lyndon B. Johnson was satisfied with Marshall's job as solicitor general. He was so satisfied that on June 13, 1967, Johnson nominated Thurgood Marshall to fill an empty spot on the Supreme Court. Marshall accepted the nomination. He would be the first African American ever to sit on the nation's highest court.

After his appointment in 1967, Thurgood Marshall continued his long battle against school segregation from the bench of the Supreme Court. In spite of the *Brown* decision in 1954, most black children in the late sixties (and even today) still went to schools where they were the large majority. The war against segregation was far from being won.

Because many southern and northern school districts resisted the *Brown* order and were slow to end segregation, the Supreme Court acted to speed up the process. Until 1968, the Court allowed local school systems to make their own plans to end segregation. In a case called *Green v. The School Board of New Kent County, Virginia* in 1968, Marshall and the other justices declared that the token efforts of school officials to desegregate were not enough. It was not enough for school boards just to have a plan to end segregation. In the *Green* case, the Court declared that it wanted results. Desegregation plans had to work. Schools had to take steps to eliminate the segregation that was already there, whether or not the school board had caused it.

The Supreme Court of the United States

The Supreme Court of the United States has made many civil rights decisions. It sometimes makes decisions that change those made earlier. In 1896, the Court made segregation legal with *Plessy* v. *Ferguson*. In *Brown* v. *Board of Education, Topeka, Kansas*, the Court made segregation illegal in American schools. In 1971, the Court ruled that lower district courts could order busing to integrate public schools. So, black children could be bused to all-white public schools and vice versa. Then in 1974, the Court ruled that children could not be bused from the city to the suburbs and vice versa. In many areas, most blacks lived in the city, while many of the whites lived in the suburbs. So this decision meant that many children would continue to attend segregated schools.

The 1990 United States Supreme Court. Associate Justice Marshall is in the front left.

Thurgood Marshall joined the U.S. Supreme Court in 1967.

In the late 1980s, Associate Justice Thurgood Marshall spoke for the need for stronger civil rights protection.

In 1971, the Court went even further. In a case called *Swann* v. *The Charlotte-Mecklenburg Board of Education*, the Court declared—again unanimously—that U.S. district courts had the power to order desegregation and could make plans on their own to integrate school systems. Most controversial, the Court declared that district courts could use buses to end segregation. If it had to, a district court could bus black children to white schools and white children to black schools. In this way, the Court hoped to end segregation in schools once and for all.

Many people opposed this decision, though. Many white parents in both the North and the South were afraid to send their children to school in neighborhoods far from home. Many black parents also feared sending their children to white neighborhoods, even though most of them supported desegregation. Having lived separated for so long, blacks and whites hardly knew one another. Because they didn't know each other, they believed many of the bad things they heard about one another and were afraid for their children.

Following these cases, district courts began ordering busing in many cities to eliminate segregation, "root and branch." The outcry from the public in these cities was often very angry and frustrated. Once again, many white parents refused to send their children to public schools. They sent them to local religious or private schools to keep them from going to school with black children.

In 1972, President Richard M. Nixon openly attacked busing and the efforts of the Court to desegregate schools. He appointed Lewis Powell and William Rehnquist, two more conservative judges, to the Supreme Court. With their influence on the Court, in 1974, the Supreme Court struck down the district court plan for desegregation in Detroit. In a case called *Milliken* v. *Bradley*, the Supreme Court ruled that the lower courts could not fight citywide school segregation by busing children between the suburbs and the city. In cities where many blacks lived in the city center and most whites lived in the suburbs, the courts could do little. Schools would remain mostly white or mostly black.

Justice Marshall wrote about the *Milliken* decision, "In the short run, it may seem to be the easier course to allow our great metropolitan areas to be divided up into two cities—one white, the other black—but it is a course, I predict, our people will ultimately regret. . . . [It is] a giant step backwards."

While busing had succeeded in ending complete segregation in some cities in the late 1980s, most African Americans still go to schools that are mostly attended by blacks or other minority groups. Most white children go to schools where there are almost no blacks. The resistance of white politicians and public, in both the North and the South, still stands as a barrier to Thurgood Marshall's dream of nonsegregated schools.

In other areas, the Supreme Court has retreated from its strong stance on civil rights. Many Americans feel the Court has gone far enough in enforcing the Constitution's guarantee of equal justice. Thurgood Marshall does not think so, and he has continued to argue for liberty and equality.

In 1978, the Supreme Court declared in *The Regents of the University of California* v. *Bakke* that colleges could not give preference to the applicants of any race when making admissions decisions. The special admissions program at the university had been designed to make up for past discrimination. According to the Court, this was unlawful. The majority of justices ruled that by giving preference to a number of minority students, the university discriminated against individual whites.

Justice Marshall disagreed strongly. He felt that the *Bakke* decision brought the Court back full circle to the days before the *Brown* case. He wrote,

> for several hundred years, Negroes have been discriminated against because of the color of their skins...[No black person,] regardless of wealth or position, has managed to escape its impact. The experience of Negroes in

America has been different in kind, not just in degree, from that of other ethnic groups. It is not merely the history of slavery alone but also that a whole people were marked as inferior by the law.... The dream of America as the great melting pot has not been realized for the Negro; because of his skin color he never even made it into the pot....

From his position on the Supreme Court, Marshall continued to speak out for civil rights, urging young people to use the law and not violence to change the way they were treated. On May 4, 1969, he spoke to the students of Dillard University in New Orleans. He had no speech prepared, just some notes. He said,

...Nothing will be settled with a gun. Nothing will be settled with a fire bomb. And nothing will be settled with a rock.... People say, "Well, at last we've got recognition. At last the country knows our problem...." If it is recognized then what? Work toward it in a lawful manner.... It takes no courage to get in the back of a crowd and throw a rock. Rather, it takes courage to stand up on your two feet and look anyone straight in the eye and say, "I will not be beaten." I say to you... Move, but move within the Constitution, and find new ways of moving nonviolently within the Constitution, bearing in mind that there are many of us in this country who will not let it go down the drain.

In 1971, an artist named Reuben Kramer was selected from among 45 artists to build a statue of Thurgood Marshall. It took Kramer almost two years to complete the nine-foot-tall bronze statue. "If there was an inspiration for the statue," said Kramer, "it was that Marshall grew from the slums of West Baltimore to the heights of the Supreme Court. That's why the statue is so straight and tall... it shows him like a great oak tree.... Below the knees, it looks like a tree...then it sort of grows into a human being." Kramer was hired to build the statue in honor of the 100th anniversary of the Bar Association of Baltimore City. Of course, when a young man named Thurgood Marshall became a lawyer, no African Americans were allowed into the Bar Association. Now one sits on the Supreme Court. The country has indeed changed.

Marshall believes that although the United States is a better, friendlier nation for blacks, there is still much room for growth. "Take it from me," he says, "we haven't won yet. We have a long way to go.... You may tell the other side for me, look out... I don't give up. I ain't even thinking about it."

In the more than 20 years that Marshall has sat on the Supreme Court, he has been a voice of freedom and liberty for all people. In 1987, when the United States celebrated the 200th anniversary of the Constitution, Marshall was especially outspoken. While most of the country was gearing up for a huge party, Marshall asked the people of the United States to remember that the original Constitution did not provide for the rights of blacks or women. In a speech before a law association in Hawaii, Marshall said that "the true miracle of the Constitution was not its birth but its life."

Many were angered by Marshall's speech. Supreme Court justices were not supposed to publicly voice their private opinions. In response to a reporter who was critical of his outspokenness, Marshall said, "Maybe he can forget about slavery. I can't, and I don't ever intend to forget it."

In the past few years, the U.S. Supreme Court has decided many cases that critics say are not in the best interest of civil rights. In most of these cases, laws were overturned or changed. In one case, white firefighters in Birmingham, Alabama, were told it was legal to sue a company that had a policy of hiring blacks or other minorities first. In another case, the Court struck down a civil rights law. The law made construction companies working for a city government put aside some money especially for hiring minorities to do part of the work. In a six-to-three decision, the Court said this was no longer necessary.

Thurgood Marshall was one of the three justices who did not agree with the decision.

Marshall knows that there are many who would like him and his views on civil rights off the Supreme Court. In 1981, a 73-year-old Marshall was called by *The New York Times* and asked if there was any truth to the rumor that he was retiring from the Court. "It's a lie," responded Marshall. "My secretary denied it to the man who started it before he started it."

At age 79, Marshall was so tired of being asked about retirement that he told a reporter for *Life*, "I was appointed for life and I intend to serve out my term."

Thurgood Marshall is not a well man. He has hearing problems and weight problems and eye problems and a lung disease. He quit a three-pack-a-day cigarette habit in 1976 after a mild heart attack. But he is serious about serving out his term. Now in his 80s, Thurgood Marshall is not about to give up his spot on the bench to a justice who does not feel as strongly as he does about civil rights. He has fought this battle too long to back down as long as he thinks he is needed in the fight.

There was a time when Marshall moved quietly to the back of a bus and then won the right not to have to in the courtroom. There was a time he was called a "nigger" and chose to stick his constitutional rights in his back pocket. Without this sense of there being an appropriate time and place for everything, Marshall would not have won the giant battles against racism that he did. To many, the *Brown* case Marshall argued in 1954 and 1955 was the most important Supreme Court decision ever made. Louis H. Pollak, the former dean of the Yale Law School, said that "except for waging and winning the Civil War and World Wars I and II, the decision [of *Brown* v. *Board of Education*] was probably the most important American governmental act of any kind since [Lincoln freed the slaves]." Marshall agrees. "Because of my participation [in the case]," he said, "I perhaps could overestimate *Brown*'s importance. I doubt it though."

Because Marshall spent so much time in the courtroom, he was sometimes asked by the youth of America to stand up for his decision to fight legal battles instead of those on the street. But the issue was always a crystal-clear one for Marshall. When a young man came up to him once and said: "...Before I listen to you I want to know: Were you in Selma?" Marshall replied, "Have [I] been! I was in Selma. Not with a whole lot of troops protecting me. I was there with nobody but a lawyer from Birmingham and me, all by our lonesome in a car, at a time when [your] father was scared to move out of the house."

In the opinion of many Americans, Thurgood Marshall is one of the most important men who has ever lived. Using the law and the U.S. Constitution, he laid down the blueprints for great change in the United States. Many of the legal battles he fought and the civil rights he won still affect Americans today. As late as 1989, the Topeka Board of Education was taken to court for not following the laws set down in the *Brown* case.

The civil rights movement was a child of many parents, from Martin Luther King, Jr., to Rosa Parks, to little Linda Brown. But in the courtrooms of Washington, one man did more to change the laws that had stripped African Americans of their freedom than anyone else. Thurgood Marshall helped to make the blacks of the United States part of "We the People." When asked how he would like to be remembered, Marshall said he would like people to say, "He did the best he could with what he had."

Timetable of Events
in the Life of
Thurgood Marshall

July 2, 1908	Born to Norma Arica and William Canfield Marshall
1925–29	Attends Lincoln University, Pennsylvania
1929	Marries Vivian (Buster) Burey
1929–33	Attends Howard University Law School in Washington, D.C. Graduated at the head of the class
1933	Begins practicing law in Baltimore, Maryland
1936	Begins working for National Association for the Advancement of Colored People (NAACP) as assistant special counsel
1938	Becomes chief counsel for NAACP
1940–61	Serves as the first director and chief counsel for newly formed NAACP Legal Defense Fund
1955	Marries Cecilia S. Suyat (Sissy); later had two children—Thurgood, Jr., and John
1961–65	Appointed judge on the United States Court of Appeals, Second Circuit, by President John F. Kennedy
1965	Appointed solicitor general, Department of Justice, by President Lyndon B. Johnson
1967– present	Serves as first African American to be an associate justice on United States Supreme Court (appointed by President Lyndon B. Johnson)

SUGGESTED READING

Bland, Randall W. *Private Pressure on Public Law: The Legal Career of Justice Thurgood Marshall*. Port Washington, NY and London: National University Publications and Kennikat Press, 1973.

Branch, Taylor. *Parting the Waters: America in the King Years 1954–63*. New York: Simon and Schuster, 1988.

*Feinberg, Barbara Silberdick. *The Constitution Yesterday, Today, and Tomorrow*. New York: Scholastic, 1978.

*Fenderson, Lewis H. *Thurgood Marshall: Fighter for Justice*. McGraw-Hill and Rutledge Books, 1969.

*Hughes, Langston. *Famous American Negroes*. New York: Dodd Mead, 1954.

Joseph, Joel D. *Black Mondays: Worst Decisions of the Supreme Court*. Bethesda: National Press, 1987.

Morris, Aldon. *The Origins of the Civil Rights Movement*. New York: The Free Press, 1984.

Quarles, Benjamin. *The Negro in the Making of America*. New York: Macmillan, 1987.

Rehnquist, William H. *The Supreme Court: How It Was, How It Is*. New York: William Morrow, 1987.

Williams, Juan. *Eyes on the Prize: America's Civil Rights Years 1954–1965*. New York: Viking, 1987.

*Readers of *Thurgood Marshall: Changing the Legal System* will find these books particularly readable.

SOURCES

BOOKS

Bland, Randall W. *Private Pressure on Public Law: The Legal Career of Justice Thurgood Marshall*. Port Washington, NY and London: National University Publications and Kennikat Press, 1973.

Branch, Taylor. *Parting the Waters: America in the King Years 1954–63*. New York: Simon and Schuster, 1988.

Feinberg, Barbara Silberdick. *The Constitution Yesterday, Today and Tomomrrow*. New York: Scholastic, 1978.

Fenderson, Lewis II. *Thurgood Marshall: Fighter for Justice*. McGraw-Hill and Rutledge Books, 1969.

Hughes, Langston. *Famous American Negroes*. New York: Dodd Mead, 1954.

Joseph, Joel D. *Black Mondays: Worst Decisions of the Supreme Court*. Bethesda: A Zenith Edition National Press, 1987.

Low, W.A. and Virgil A. Clift, eds. *Encyclopedia of Black America*. New York: McGraw-Hill, 1981.

MacKenzie, John P., Leon Friedman, and Fred L. Israel, eds. *The Justices of the United States Supreme Court 1789–1969: Their Lives and Major Opinions Volume IV* (Thurgood Marshall pgs. 3068–3108). New York and London: Chelsea House and R.R. Bowker, 1969.

Metcalf, George R. *Black Profiles*. New York: McGraw-Hill, 1970.

Morris, Aldon. *The Origins of the Civil Rights Movement*. New York: The Free Press, 1984.

Murphy, Walter F. and C. Herman Pritchett. *Courts, Judges and Politics: An Introduction to the Judicial Process (Third Edition)*. New York: Random House, 1979.

Quarles, Benjamin. *The Negro in the Making of America*. New York: Macmillan, 1987.

Rehnquist, William H. *The Supreme Court: How It Was, How It Is*. New York: William Morrow, 1987.

Robinson, Wilhemina S. *Historical Afro-American Biographies*. International Library of Afro-American Life and History, 1979 Edition. Cornwall Heights, PA: The Publishers Agency, 1978.

Williams, Juan. *Eyes on the Prize: America's Civil Rights Years 1954–1965*. New York: Viking, 1984.

The Concise Columbia Encyclopedia. New York: Columbia University Press, 1983.

The Ebony Success Library Volume II: Famous Blacks Give Secrets of Success. Chicago: Johnson Publishing, 1973.

The Supreme Court Justice and the Law. Congressional Quarterly, Inc., Washington, D.C., 1983.

The World Almanac and Book of Facts. New York: Pharos Books, 1989.

MAGAZINE ARTICLES

Zion, Sidney, "Thurgood Marshall Takes a New Tush-Tush Job." *New York Times Magazine*, August 22, 1965.

"Mr. Justice Marshall." *Newsweek*, June 26, 1967.

"A Supreme Court Justice's Warning to Fellow Negroes." *U.S. News and World Report*, May 19, 1969.

"With Mr. Marshall on the Supreme Court." *U.S. News and World Report*, June 26, 1967.

"Thurgood Marshall." *Time*, September 19, 1955.

INDEX

Alabama, University of, 83, 86
American Bar Association (ABA), 34

Baltimore and Ohio railroad, 20
Belden, Stanley, 49–54
Bergman, Walter, 96
Black Mondays, 9
Blackjack, 51
Bloody Sunday, 102
Boycott, 79–82
Bradley, Mamie, 78
Briggs, Harry, 63–64, 70
Briggs, Liza, 64
Brown, Linda, 69
Brown, Minniejean, 89
Brown, Oliver, 69
Brown v. *Board of Education of Topeka*, 70–75, 108, 114–115
Bryant, Carolyn, 77
Bus boycott, 79–82

Carter, Robert, 64
Central High School, Little Rock, 86–90
Cheatwood, Vernon, 51–52, 54–55
Civil Rights Act (1964), 99, 101–102
Civil rights law, 31
Civil War, 10
Clark, Kenneth B., 64–66
Colclasure, E.O., 51–52, 54
Constitution, 7–9, 10
Constitutional amendments, 10–11
  13th, 10
  14th, 10, 59, 72, 106
  15th, 10–11
Court of Appeals, U.S., 95

Davis, John W., 70–71, 72
Debating, 24–25
Dexter Avenue Baptist Church, Montgomery, 68
Dillard University, 112
Dred Scott case, 9–10
Du Bois, W. E. B., 27

Durr, Clifford, 79

Eckford, Elizabeth, 87–88
Eisenhower, Dwight D., 72, 88–89
Emancipation Proclamation, 10

Faubus, Orval, 87, 89, 90
Fifteenth Amendment, 10–11
Fourteenth Amendment, 10, 59, 72, 106
Freedom Riders, 95–98

Gaines, Lloyd Lionel, 39–41, 42, 55, 59
Gandhi, Mohandas, 81
Gibbs, William 43
Green, Ernest, 89
Green v. *School Board of New Kent County, Virginia*, 107
Grooms, Judge, 86

Hamer, Fannie Lou, 12
Harmon, Roy, 52–53
Harvard Law Review, 32
Harvard University, 28, 32
Hazing, 24
Horton, Norman, 53–54
Houston, Charles Hamilton, 29, 32–35, 38, 39–41, 60, 73
Howard University, 28–36, 92

Integration of movie house, 26–27

Jet magazine, 78
Jim Crow laws, 37–38, 43, 81–82
Johns, Barbara Rose, 66–68, 70
Johns, Vernon, 68
Johnson, Lyndon B., 6, 7, 101, 102, 107
Johnson, Mordecai, 29

Kennedy, John F., 98, 99, 101, 105
Kilpatrick, James J., 95
King, Martin Luther, Jr., 8, 12, 81, 91, 98–100, 103, 105
Kramer, Reuben, 112

Ku Klux Klan, 106

Lincoln, Abraham, 10
Lincoln University, 23–28, 40, 42
Little Rock, Arkansas, schools
    desegrated, 86–90
Little Rock Nine, 87, 89
Lucy, Authurine J., 83, 86
Lynchings, 17, 75–78, 85
Lyons, W. D., 49–55

McLaurin, G. W., 57–59
Madrid, University of, 32
Malcolm X, 12
March
    in Birmingham, 98–99
    from Selma to Montgomery,
        102–103
    on Washington, 99–101
Margold, Nathan Ross, 38
Margold Report, 38
Marshall, Aubrey (brother), 15
Marshall, Cecilia Suyat (second
    wife), 91
Marshall, John (son), 91
Marshall, Norma Arica (mother),
    13, 16
Marshall, Thoroughgood
    (grandfather), 13–14
Marshall, Thurgood
    and *Bakke* case, 111–112
    born, 13
    and *Brown* v. *Board of Education of
        Topeka*, 70–75, 114–115
    and bus boycott, 81–82
    childhood, 16–22
    as Court of Appeals judge, 94–95
    and desegregation at Little Rock,
        86–90
    and *Gaines* case, 39–41
    and *Gibbs* case, 43
    at Howard University, 28–36
    and integration of movie house,
        26–27
    joins NAACP staff, 38
    as lawyer for common people,
        46–47
    at Lincoln University, 23–28
    and *McLaurin* case, 57–59
    marries Cecilia Suyat, 91

marries Vivien Burey, 28
and *Murray* case, 39
named Supreme Court justice, 7,
    107
and *Pan of Bones* case, 49–55
and *Plessy* v. *Ferguson*, 59–60
in private practice, 36
and sit-ins, 91–92
as solicitor general, 6–7, 105–107
sons are born, 91
and *Sweatt* case, 56–57, 59
Marshall, Thurgood Jr. (son), 91
Marshall, Vivien Burey (Buster)
    (first wife), 28, 45, 75
Marshall, William Canfield (father)
    13, 16
Maryland, University of, 28, 39
Michigan, University of, 42
Milliken v. *Bradley*, 110–111
Missouri, University of, 39–41, 42
Montgomery Advertiser, 78, 80
Montgomery bus boycott, 79–82
Montgomery Improvement
    Association (MIA), 81
Moton High School, 66–68
Murray, Donald Gaines, 39, 55, 59

Nabrit, James, 33, 60
National Association for the
    Advancement of Colored
    People (NAACP), 17, 35, 36,
    37, 38, 41, 43, 56, 61
    Legal Defense Fund, 43, 60–61,
        75, 88, 91
National Negro Committee, 17
National Review magazine, 95
New York Times, 114
New York Times Magazine, 46, 95
Nixon, E. D., 79–80
Nixon, Richard M., 110

Oklahoma, University of, 57

Pan of Bones case, 49–55
Parks, Rosa, 78–80
Plessy, Homer, 12
Plessy v. *Ferguson*, 12, 38, 59–60, 108
Pollak, Louis H., 114
Poll taxes, 103
Pound, Roscoe, 32

About the Author

Debra Hess is a Boston University graduate who specializes in writing for children. She has spent three years as an editor for a nationwide newspaper for students and has contributed plays, interviews, and stories for publications in the United States and England, including two highly acclaimed short plays on Martin Luther King, Jr.